Becoming Deliberate

T0163719

There are many journeys we take on the road to becoming and accepting our authentic self. The journeys are littered with off ramps best remembered and rest stops that can rejuvenate the traveler. *Becoming Deliberate* and Cheryl Bonini Ellis are two companions we all need to reach our next destination more enlightened and uplifted!

—**Karen L. Ball**, President and CEO,
The Sturge-Weber Foundation, www.sturge-weber.org

Leadership has now a clear, grounded and inspiring framework.

If you want to be **an authentic leader** then *Becoming Deliberate* is for you.

—**Jill Douka**, #1 Bestselling Author of *Choose Love*,
International Speaker, www.jilldouka.com

I always count on Cheryl Bonini Ellis for her wisdom and balanced perspective. In *Becoming Deliberate*, she shares strategies for achieving both on the path to becoming a more effective and fulfilled leader. I highly recommend this powerful book for everyone who aspires to leading a life by design, not by default.

—**Sheri Fink**, #1 Best-selling, Award-Winning Author,
President of "The Whimsical World of Sheri Fink"
Inspirational Brand, and International Speaker

Leading yourself allows you to lead others. If you are ready to "become the lighthouse in the fog" as Cheryl Ellis so eloquently puts it, this quick-read book will give you the practical next steps you need to make that happen.

—**Anne C. Graham**, Author,
Profit In Plain Sight, and Speaker of the Year.

In *Becoming Deliberate*, Cheryl Ellis clearly lays out what's needed for leaders leading in an increasing complex, diverse and ambiguous world. Doing the tough inside work is the missing ingredient. An awesome leadership development guide for leaders who want to enlist and engage their teams and their customers.

—**Cheryl Liew-Chng**, CEO LifeWorkz, Creator of
The 24-Hour Woman,™ International Speaker,
Author & Strategist on Talent Innovation,
Diversity & Inclusion, Work Life Flexibility & Leadership

What a wealth of information! I loved your numerous references to other books, quotes by other leaders, and facts (especially about the economy). Your personal stories were very engaging — and endearing.

You teach us how to WIN at our own mind games. I especially appreciated the clear-cut steps for reaching certain objectives.

And everyone needs to be constantly asking themselves "What do I WANT?"!!

—**Angela Margolit**, President,
Bluebird Auto Rental Systems, LP, www.barsnet.com

Cheryl Ellis takes you on a journey to transform the way you think about leadership in your work and in your life. She masterfully guides you on how to shift your thinking and offers brilliant actions steps to make you a more committed and effective leader. If you want to become the best version of yourself and lead on purpose, this book is for you.

—**Karen Murphy**, Executive Director,
Pro-Tec Building Restoration Services, Inc.

Becoming Deliberate is the long awaited missing link to create a healthier DNA in every organization. Cheryl Ellis's insights in leading, from a more feminine standpoint, would decrease abuse of power and greed thinking, and move toward embracing the next generation, while keeping it ethical and authentic. Her messages applied are making the world a more beautiful living and working place in our human society.

—**Michael W. Payne**, Aesthetic Plastic Surgeon, Birmingham and London, UK

Becoming Deliberate resonates with leadership qualities and tactics so sought and often lacking today, it was a pleasure seeing a map of the process to get there in print.

By focusing on a leader's inner journey, Cheryl Bonini Ellis reminds us to Live, Love, Learn, and Laugh. Delving deeper, the author invites us to examine our choices and where we have - and need to build - further spheres of influence. Here, she states, anyone can be a leader. And so you are!

Leadership begins with a single person, YOU. This book gives you several frameworks and perspectives from which to consider your direction as a leader. Where will you head? Engage in *Becoming Deliberate* and decide!

—**Dr Wayne Pernell**, Amazon Best-Selling Author and Hay House Featured Author, High Performance Leadership Coach, www.WaynePernell.com

I can't imagine anyone who would not benefit from reading this book. As Cheryl Bonini Ellis points out, in the 21st century you don't need to hold a title to be leader. You must, however, understand how to influence your own thoughts and emotions—and those of other people.

Ellis climbed the corporate-banking ladder at a time when female role models were nearly nonexistent. Thus she began her independent, lifelong study of leadership, reading voraciously on the subject, and always taking notes of what others around her did well or not so well. "I never wanted to be the kind of leader that left people feeling the way I felt much of the time—underestimated, unappreciated, and underutilized."

After decades of keen observations, plus hands-on experience coaching C-suite execs, Ellis has created this gem. Whether you're a parent, teacher, or CEO, this book will teach you how to lead effectively, providing clear strategies, exercises and examples along the way. It will shift your perspective on leadership in general, and very possibly change your life.

—**Jane Ransom**, CEO Jane Ransom Enterprises, www.janeransom.com

In order to be an effective leader of others, one must first do the work to find and embrace their inner voice. This will then lead to authenticity and credibility, two critical keys to leadership. In this outstanding book, Cheryl gives you the tools to find your voice and shares insights from her own journey and those of others that you will find insightful and inspiring.

—**Ruth Ross**, Engagement Evangelist, Speaker & Author of *Coming Alive: The Journey To Reengage Your Life And Career*

If you want to improve your abilities as a leader, or become a leader, this book will give you the tools you need to make you a leader of influence. The tools to change your thinking to right thinking and the perspective to ask the right questions that determine how impactful you are as a leader.

—**Laura Steward**, award winning author of *What Would a Wise Woman Do?*, International Speaker and Business Strategist.

Becoming Deliberate

Changing the Game of Leadership
from the Inside Out

Cheryl Bonini Ellis

New York

Becoming Deliberate
Changing the Game of Leadership from the Inside Out

Published in New York, New York, by Morgan James Publishing. Morgan James and The Entrepreneurial Publisher are trademarks of Morgan James, LLC. www.MorganJamesPublishing.com

The Morgan James Speakers Group can bring authors to your live event. For more information or to book an event visit The Morgan James Speakers Group at www.TheMorganJamesSpeakersGroup.com.

A **free** eBook edition is available with the purchase of this print book.

ISBN 978-1-63047-403-4 paperback
ISBN 978-1-63047-404-1 eBook
ISBN 978-1-63047-405-8 hardcover
Library of Congress Control Number:
2014948856

CLEARLY PRINT YOUR NAME ABOVE IN UPPER CASE

Instructions to claim your free eBook edition:
1. Download the BitLit app for Android or iOS
2. Write your name in **UPPER CASE** on the line
3. Use the BitLit app to submit a photo
4. Download your eBook to any device

Cover Design by:
John Weber

Interior Design by:
Bonnie Bushman
bonnie@caboodlegraphics.com

In an effort to support local communities and raise awareness and funds, Morgan James Publishing donates a percentage of all book sales for the life of each book to Habitat for Humanity Peninsula and Greater Williamsburg.

Get involved today, visit
www.MorganJamesBuilds.com

Habitat
for Humanity®
Peninsula and
Greater Williamsburg
Building Partner

Dedication

This book is dedicated to

Denny,
The love of my life and the one who keeps me [somewhat] grounded
Life with you – what an adventure!

My Parents
With profound gratitude for the core values and healthy genes.

My sister Cindy
For her unfailing sense of humor.
I will always love you.

My brother Eddie
Wish you were here.
Thank you for the daily guidance and inspiration.

Table of Contents

Acknowledgments

Writing a book has been a transformative experience beyond anything I expected. It would not have happened without a series of events and many supportive characters. During my thirty years growing up in the world of business, people often told me "you should write a book," and I thank them for planting the seed.

The reality developed while attending Jack Canfield's Breakthrough to Success program and established writing a book as my "breakthrough" goal. Thank you to my Mastermind Team, Jane, Jill, Sheri, Yeliv and Winston, still going strong after four years, for helping me keep this dream alive.

As I was creating an audio training program called *Essential Leadership Thinking*, my business coach, Jennifer Hines, encouraged me with "Cheryl, you have a book here." I am grateful to Jennifer for so many reasons, not the least of which has been her unfailing encouragement throughout this process. Jennifer, Chapter 8 is dedicated to you for always challenging me with the right questions at the right time.

One day on a Skype call with my fellow Center Ring Member, Wolfgang Payne, he challenged me to beat the year-end deadline for submitting my book proposal to Morgan James. Thanks to Wolfgang, I made good on the challenge. And Wolfgang continued to support me with critical feedback all along the way. I truly value his perspective.

My inspiration for this book came from many of the leaders I have been fortunate to work with throughout my career in financial services, many of whom served as models of "what not to do."

Since leaving corporate life, a series of coaches and mentors have taught me much, have challenged my thinking and raised my level of ambition about my ability to contribute. I am grateful to Brad Sugars, Keith Cunningham, Jack Canfield, John C. Maxwell, Roger Love and Bo Eason.

I am especially grateful to Brendon Burchard, who always challenges me to be the best possible version of me. It has been a true privilege to be part of his Center Ring, a Mastermind of smart, committed professionals, each of whom wants to use his or her expertise to make the world a better place. I am constantly inspired by their good work. And each of them has contributed to this project with constant encouragement and support.

For their willingness to transform their work and their lives, I appreciate the special clients whose stories have been told here. Working on yourself is not easy; it takes courage and commitment and I am so proud of their continual progress. A special note of appreciation to Karen Murphy for always supporting my various projects, including this one, with useful, specific feedback – you make everything better!

To Betty Rengifo Uribe, thanks for working to make the world a better place and for sharing the story of your inspiring journey with me. To the other amazing women and men who have incredible life stories, even though I only shared a snippet, please keep up the good work! We need you.

Starting with Rick Frishman, brother Scott, and David Hancock, the people at Morgan James Publishing have been phenomenal partners. They are dedicated to the success of their authors and make the process comfortable, with great support every step of the way.

Speaking of partners, this book would not be what it is without the incredible guidance and support of Justin Spizman, book architect par excellence. He not only helped me convey my message, but also challenged my thinking and pushed me to express myself fully and openly. He seemed to understand me instantly and then, encouraged me every step of the way. He is truly one of a kind and working with him helped to make this experience a true pleasure for me.

Thanks to Angie Kiesling, who performed the final edit with such an extraordinary eye for detail. To say she is thorough is an understatement.

John Weber of j.weber creative worked with me through multiple iterations of the book cover design. His creativity and flexibility and desire to "get it right" have always been an inspiration to me as we've collaborated frequently over the years. Thank you John for all you have done.

This book is dedicated to my close friends and family members, who have always supported me no matter how crazy I get with ideas and schemes and hopes and dreams. And, as importantly, they keep me laughing. I love you all very much, including those of you who are only with me in spirit.

Denny, thank you for always being there in big and small ways. Life is so much easier when you know someone has your back.

With bottomless gratitude, I acknowledge your contributions to this project—and to me.

Dear Reader

Dear Reader,

The need for effective leadership is now greater than ever. Given the ever-escalating pace of change, the expansion of technology, and the growing realization that competition comes from every corner, we are becoming more immersed in a world of increasing complexity filled with unknowns. Furthermore, demographics are dramatically changing. The days of a single-generation workforce are long gone. Consider, for example, the fact that today we have four distinct generations working side by side—or sometimes virtually. Each of these unique groups carries distinct needs, values, and communication preferences. Thus, leadership practices are shifting and moving in a drastically different direction. What was once the gold standard in leadership behavior is now outdated and seemingly obsolete.

All these factors point to a growing need for thoughtful and considerate leaders at *every* level of *every* organization. Effective leadership has become a game of inches. The companies with strong cultures and strong leadership often gain those inches. The ones that don't often fall short and succumb to the competition. The difference between an adaptable and engaged leader and one caught in the past can mean the difference between a successful, flourishing company and one that decays from within.

Historically, leaders could rely on their position or title to command and control the actions of others and drive toward a result. Today's leaders need to cultivate a level of influence by building connections that develop trust and inspire followers. And the leaders of the future will be those who are adept at developing other leaders throughout their circle of influence. It literally takes a "village" to introduce and inject strong leadership into a growing company. From the CEO to management and throughout the organization, leadership is a team effort and one that I have studied, learned, and implemented for professionals and companies across a wide range of industries.

I have worked in various leadership roles throughout the business world for more than forty years. During that time I have personally experienced the ever-changing landscape of leadership and the requirements for leading a team effectively. And what I've observed is that building leadership ability and credibility is a lifelong process. In fact, the very best leaders work at it consistently and intentionally. The best also know that leadership emanates from the inside out. It all starts with the right thinking and the right mindset.

In writing this book, my purpose is to enhance leadership practices in the business world by developing leaders from the inside out that are authentic, energetic, respectful, and inspirational. My mission is to provide insight and perspective, combined with training and development to business leaders that will enable them to get better results while making a bigger impact as leaders.

Becoming Deliberate will challenge your thinking about leadership and shift it toward a more thoughtful, intentional way of leading. Peter Drucker, whose writings contributed to the philosophical and practical foundations of the modern business world, said, "Leadership is lifting a person's vision to high sights, the raising of a person's performance to a higher standard, the building of a personality beyond its normal limitations." Together we will journey down the path of mindful and purposeful leadership and examine the practice of setting high benchmarks for your company and exceeding them through innovative leadership practices.

This book will offer a tangible perspective on how your thinking influences your leadership ability and credibility, together with valuable insight and guidance that elevates your own thinking about leadership. As you read, you will understand more clearly the need to take control of your mindset. And by implementing the strategies and tactics I describe, you will improve not only your own ability to lead but also your ability to influence and inspire others to lead.

I am excited to be your guide on this journey.

Cheryl Bonini Ellis

Chapter 1

The Case for Leadership:
Does It Really Matter?

The greatest revolution of our generation is the discovery that human beings, by changing the inner attitudes of their minds, can change the outer aspects of their lives.
—Harvard psychologist **William James**

E ffective leadership starts with the right thinking and the right mindset.

This book will teach you how to build the critical foundation that must be in place before you can lead others to great success. It will challenge how you think about the notion of leadership. It will help you to recognize the detriment of negative thinking and teach you how to deactivate it and transform your thinking—and your leadership.

Ultimately, it will help to shape your inner voice from one filled with doubt to one that projects strength and support to your team.

As a result of implementing this improved mindset, new thought process, and better habits, you will find yourself more confident in your leadership ability as you quickly gain more credibility as a leader. You will improve your ability to connect with others and influence them. All this will lead to better results and more meaningful impact as a leader.

Reaching the ultimate level of leadership is directly connected with what you stand for and what you represent. In other words, it is more about *who you are* than what you do. And who you are starts with *how you think*. *Becoming Deliberate* will help you think like—and become—a more effective and more influential leader.

In the movie *The Iron Lady*, starring Meryl Streep as Margaret Thatcher, the first woman prime minister of Great Britain (who held that post the longest of anyone in the twentieth century) was paraphrasing Mahatma Gandhi when she said:

Our **thoughts** become our **words**.
Our **words** become our **actions**.
Our **actions** become our **habits**.
Our **habits** form our **character** and
Our **character** ultimately becomes our **destiny**.

The power of your thoughts to control your destiny is profound. It is the reason so many bestselling books on the subject have been written, and then read over and over again by those in managerial and leadership positions. They do this to ultimately take advantage of their thinking and to support the success in their lives. Together, we will take a very similar but unique journey to architect a more impactful and meaningful destiny.

The power of your thoughts to control your destiny is profound.

Evolution of Leadership

Over the past four decades, both the nature and requirements of leadership have dramatically changed. Once upon a time, business leaders relied solely on their positions or titles or other credentials to effect change or to direct the actions of others. They didn't expect to be questioned or challenged, only obeyed. Mostly, everyone worked under one roof where they could be closely watched and managed.

Managers were required to set and then communicate expectations, hold team members accountable for their actions, and provide feedback on their performance. Most of that feedback consisted of pointing out mistakes and requesting improvement. Developmental goals were set and monitored. More feedback was offered to fix what was perceived as broken.

It became more challenging for leaders as the workforce expanded to include more women and different cultures. They needed their teams to buy into the vision and work together collaboratively. Sometimes those teams were geographically dispersed, which made clear and consistent communication more difficult. Leaders were required to attend diversity training, aimed at helping them to understand and "value" differences so that they could identify and leverage strengths and avoid offensive behavior. Almost overnight, leadership became extremely complicated.

Today, leaders who attempt to rely on the "position" type of leadership that worked in the past rarely succeed to move others to action. The typical response is that most workers do only the minimum required and often with a poor attitude, leaving work as soon as they are able. Productivity suffers, customer service is lacking, and turnover remains high.

Workers today have higher expectations from their work and from their leaders. They want recognition, appreciation, and the opportunity to learn and grow. They look for purpose and fulfillment at their place of employment and become disengaged and uninterested when it is not delivered upon. They want to make a difference. They want a positive work/life balance. And they will not stay where they do not get what they desire.

As a result, it takes much more *intention* and *attention* for leaders to provide the type of motivational environment where people have a desire to perform at their best. Team members have more options than ever before, and they can pursue the options more easily with the aid of a quick Internet search for new job opportunities or the use of social media to learn about the culture of an organization and whether or not it fits their needs.

In the future, leadership will continue to evolve. The expansion of technology makes working from anywhere and anytime a growing reality. This will require leaders to create crystal-clear expectations and minimize the impact of blind spots. They will need better ways to measure performance and productivity. To succeed, leaders will need to excel at providing the direction *and* the resources to support the accomplishment of goals, objectives, and the desired results.

As the world moves at the speed of light, and things keep changing all around us, leaders will find the need for more skills, greater flexibility and adaptability.

As a leader, you have access to more information than ever before in history. You have more choices and therefore more decisions to make. And when it comes to leading others, you have more responsibility too. People are looking to *you* to show them the way. And it's important to lead them deliberately, with intention, and on purpose.

As you think about the implications of this evolution for your own leadership effectiveness, it's important to recognize the lifelong nature of leadership development and be willing to commit to an ongoing, consistent, and intentional process. When you decide to commit, you will continue to evolve as a leader. The demand for effective leadership will continue to evolve as well.

Clearly, the landscape and responsibilities of leadership have changed. But, I would argue, they have changed for the better. We now play in a more flexible and creative backdrop, allowing leadership to appear in many forms. And now that you understand the challenges ahead of you as a leader, let me help you by framing a way to turn the challenges into opportunities. To fully engage and start your journey to grow into an impactful leader, consider the fabric that makes up our new-age leaders. These four key concepts will provide a basis for the way you look at the most important work of leaders:

Keys to the Most Important Work of Leaders

The Inside Work Is the Most Important Work **1**	Self-Control: The Essential Leadership Ability **2**
3 Being Proactive, Deliberate & 100% Responsible	**4** It All Comes Down to Choice

Key #1: The Inside Work Is the Most Important Work

Your vision for yourself—and what's possible—should not be limited by your current knowledge and capabilities.
—Brendon Burchard

From my experience and observations as a business leader, and from the thought leaders I've been privileged to work with and study, the most important lesson I've learned is this: **building leadership capability requires doing the tough inside work.**

Remember, leadership is no longer about title or position. Rather, it's about *your ability to connect with others and your ability to influence others.* And since everyone has the opportunity to connect with others and to influence even one person, everyone has the opportunity to lead.

> Leadership is not about title or position. It's about your ability to connect with others and your ability to influence others.

In order to be fully effective at connecting and influencing, begin by facing the biggest leadership challenge head-on: leading yourself. In other words, you have to learn to lead from the inside out. I call this process *Learning to Lead from Within*™ and I've created a framework to guide you through the essential steps. It starts with managing your personal psychology—how you think, how you feel, and how you behave. We will explore in greater depth later on, but for now, understand that thought manifests actions and actions lead to results. Learning how to think, how to feel, and how to behave is the foundation of all leadership development.

To be a better leader you may need to learn to be a better person. Learning to be a better person is the inside work of leadership. As you master the inside work and allow that better person to shine through to the outside, you increase your ability to connect with others and influence others.

You become the lighthouse in the fog.

Here's the good news: as a leader, your biggest challenge is also your biggest opportunity. Making the investment of time, energy, and attention to improving yourself has a tremendous upside in your leadership effectiveness, your results, and the impact you can have on the lives of others.

The most effective and influential leaders realize that leadership emanates from the inside out. They understand that effective, influential leadership is an inside job. Doing the tough inside work of leadership is the most important work you will ever do, and it is an ongoing process. All change and all progress needs to start with you. More specifically, it needs to begin with the way you think. The way you think is the way you lead. Once you understand the importance of the inside work of leadership, you need to learn how to manage it, which leads us to the second key.

Key #2: Self-Control: The Essential Leadership Ability

Our life always expresses the result of our dominant thoughts.
—Soren Kierkegaard

Unless you learn to manage your thinking, your thoughts may end up managing you! We often equate self-control with managing behavior, reactions, and impulses. Thinking precedes all of these, so learning to start with your thinking will help to bring you closer to your intended result.

The way you think is the way you lead. Your mindset is more important than your skill set. When you improve the way you think, you improve the way you lead. In reality, how you think and how you influence others to think are the most essential leadership skills of all.

Did you realize that you think about seventy or eighty thousand thoughts every day? And most of these are the same thoughts you had the day before, and the day before that. What's really interesting is that research shows that about 80 percent of these thoughts are negative.

The power of your thoughts is incredible.

In 1952, forty-two-year-old Lester Levinson, a physicist and successful entrepreneur, and a man with many serious health issues, was sent home to die by his doctors. Instead, after taking on the challenge of penetrating his conscious mind and learning to let go of his inner limitations, he lived for forty-two more years. What Levinson discovered was that "we are unlimited beings, limited only by the concepts of limitation that we hold in our minds. These concepts.... are not true and because they're not true, they can be easily released or discharged."

> We are unlimited beings, limited only by the concepts of limitation that we hold in our minds. These concepts....are not true and because they're not true, they can be easily released or discharged.
>
> –Lester Levinson

Levinson's technique was eventually turned into a system that is now called The Sedona Method. It has helped hundreds of thousands of people to let go of their limiting beliefs and reduce anxiety, fear, and anger while empowering their emotional well-being.

There are countless examples of athletes and other professionals who overcame great odds or even critical injury or illness by focusing their minds on the outcome they so desired. How you think is so vital to your success at work, with relationships, and in life as a whole. Doesn't it make sense to learn how to become deliberate and intentional about your thinking?

Key #3: Being Proactive and Deliberate and 100 Percent Responsible

> *You must take personal responsibility. You cannot change the circumstances, the seasons, or the wind, but you can change yourself.*
> **—Jim Rohn**

When did you last spend time in thought? The most successful people actually schedule time to think! The third major concept representing the most important work of leaders is taking 100 percent responsibility for your thinking. That means being proactive and deliberate about *how* you think. This enables you to lead with intention and have a bigger impact as a leader.

Successful leaders agree that the most effective way to lead is by example. What is the example you are setting? What behaviors, attitudes, and thinking are you modeling for your team? And have you been *deliberate* in choosing those behaviors, attitudes, and thoughts?

Learning to be deliberate about how you think, what you think about, and what you do with what you think about will enable you to be the best role model possible. And modeling the way will lead to bigger and better results, faster and more easily. The best part is that those results will last longer and transcend time.

If you want to be successful, you need to take 100 percent responsibility for everything you experience in your life: your level of achievement, the results you produce, the quality of your relationships, the state of your health, your income, your debts, your feelings—everything!

Jack Canfield is the co-founder of the *Chicken Soup for the Soul* series. With over 225 titles in 47 languages, these books have sold more than 500 million copies. Canfield is also the author of *The Success Principles*, in which he describes the 64 principles that differentiate successful people from everyone else. His work is based on over 30 years of experience as a teacher, psychotherapist, workshop facilitator, and as founder of the Transformational Leadership Council.

Success Principle #1 is to take 100 percent responsibility for your life. This includes the acknowledgment that you create everything that happens to you and are the cause of your experiences and your results— both the successes and the failures. It means you have to give up all your excuses; all your blaming, whining, and complaining; all your "reasons"; and all your victim stories.

When you are proactive versus reactive in your thinking, it enables you to lead with intention. Deliberately taking 100 percent responsibility for your thoughts is a learned discipline, requiring commitment and practice. The benefit of creating these habits is that, once they become the default, they produce an increase in overall effectiveness, enabling you to be the best possible role model for others. And that leads us to more good news!

Key #4: It All Comes Down to Choice

Everything can be taken from a man but one thing: the last of the human freedoms—to choose one's attitude in any given set of circumstances, to choose one's own way.
—Viktor Frankl

Doing the inside work, taking control of your thoughts, and being proactive, deliberate, and 100 percent responsible for your thinking all comes down to a matter of choice. It's a decision. It's up to you. You get to choose. You can give yourself permission....or not.

As humans, we alone have the power of choice. The very thing that separates us from the rest of the animal kingdom is our ability to choose.

In *Man's Search for Meaning*, Viktor Frankl, a Holocaust survivor, writes with incredible eloquence about how he and others rose above despair, enduring daily atrocities and indignities. He experienced firsthand just how much can be taken away from a human. That is, all but his power to choose.

Choice empowers us.

Dr. Wayne Pernell wrote a wonderful book called *Choosing Your Power: Becoming who you deserve to be at home and in the world!* While he acknowledges that we live in a complex world, each facing our own set of struggles, he teaches us how to use our personal power of choice to achieve what we want. Once you recognize the things that prevent you from achieving—like fear and doubt—and those that bring you closer to your goals—like vision and determination—you can choose where to place your attention and energy.

To get the most out of any opportunity, you have to choose to do just that. If you want to improve as a leader, you have to choose to improve as a leader. You have to choose to do things differently, choose to progress and develop new skills, choose to model the way for others. You can choose your attitude, your behavior, your emotions, your beliefs, and your response to a set of circumstances. And you can choose your thoughts!

It's important to understand that before you actually *do* anything, it all starts with a thought or an idea. Your thoughts turn into actions. In other words, if it makes sense to *do* things differently, it also means you need to *think* differently.

Your ability to think differently will allow you to make the choices that will lead to the best results and the biggest impact. Don't let your lack of awareness, or your fear, or the need to be right, or the need to feel safe stand in the way of your progress. Remember, you have a choice. Here's how I learned about my own power to choose.

My Story of Choice

The most significant milestone in my life occurred when I was fifteen years old when my big brother Eddie was killed in a motorcycle accident. Although this occurred many years ago, I can still vividly recall the impact this life-altering tragedy had on my life. In an instant, I felt the world crashing down around me and I knew my life had changed forever. I felt intense anger and a profound sense of loss. I became anxious, worried about my parents, wondering how they would survive without Eddie. This significant event formed the very basis of my identity for many years following my brother's death. I desperately tried to make sense of what happened and struggled to put it into perspective.

Then, one day I realized I had been very sad for a very long time and that I was tired of being sad. I decided to be happy again. Just like that. It was a choice. And I made it. I'm not saying I've never been sad since then. I certainly have been. But I realized that I had a choice, and I could either wallow in my sadness *or* change my state of mind *and* change the way I felt. And so can you.

This is a wonderful ability that we humans possess. You too can decide. You can choose. And when you make a choice, and it is in alignment with right thinking, very often you will be rewarded with greater clarity.

For me, once I reopened the possibility of a happy life, I was rewarded with some very important life lessons that I carry with me to this day and that define the way I work and live:

1. **LIVE** in the present moment. Life can change in an instant and we may not be prepared for that. Do not sweat the small stuff.

2. **LOVE** your life and the people in it. Don't take it—or them—for granted. Bring kindness and caring into the world, and be expressive about it.

3. Seek to add value and make a difference in the life of others. The best way to do this is to **LEARN** and grow and continuously improve.

4. Remember to **LAUGH** every day. Keep your sense of humor, no matter what.

My Mantra

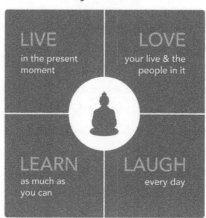

LIVE
in the present
moment

LOVE
your live & the
people in it

LEARN
as much as
you can

LAUGH
every day

Live. Love. Learn. Laugh. It's become my mantra. And, without the decision to leave my sadness behind and embrace happiness again, I might have missed it. For me, the challenge became living these messages as a young female business leader in a changing world. Now I wake up every day and choose to live, love, learn, and laugh. This is a key element of leadership. It becomes even more important when you decide to live a happy and meaningful life. Because if you remain unhappy, how can you possibly motivate and inspire others to do great things?

So with keeping these key concepts in mind, along with an in-depth understanding of the evolution and current leadership environment, we find ourselves on the cusp of reinventing not only the manner in which we view leadership, but also the way in which we lead. U.S. President John Quincy Adams said, "If your actions inspire others to dream more, learn more, do more, and become more, you are a leader."

> If your actions inspire others to dream more, learn more, do more, and become more, you are a leader.
> –John Quincy Adams

We all possess leadership qualities that reside within. And at one time or another, we will have the opportunity to set the precedent and guide others. Whether it be as a CEO, manager, boss, parent, older sibling, or even a friend, the time will come when a loved one or colleague will look to you for direction. Through learning the steadfast principles and tools of great leaders presented in this book, when that moment occurs, you will be ready to answer the call.

☞ Usable Insights

- As the landscape and responsibilities of leadership have changed, the demand for effective leadership is greater than ever and so is the opportunity for everyone to become a leader.
- Building leadership capability requires doing the tough inside work, the most important work of leaders. Learning to be a better person is both your biggest challenge and your biggest opportunity.
- The essential leadership ability is self-control, and it extends to thinking because your behavior, reactions and impulses all start there. Unless you learn to manage your thinking, your thoughts may end up managing you.

- Becoming deliberate, proactive and 100 percent responsible for your life and your thinking enables you to lead with intention and purpose.
- The power of choice is a profound enabler in your life and in your work.

Action Steps

1. Think of an area in your life where you want better results. List 3 enabling thoughts that would support you in getting those better results.
2. Choose one leadership quality that you know for sure is important. Ask yourself: how good am I at that? Identify one action you can take to improve.

Chapter 2

Transformational Leadership:
Turning Challenges into Opportunities

If you are paying attention, each and every experience you have can contribute to who you become as a leader.
—Cheryl Bonini Ellis

Most leadership journeys come with difficult choices and hard lessons. However, you will find great value in these obstacles once you begin to honor the journey, the struggle, and the educational process. When you truly appreciate the contributions of every experience, the benefit to your growth and development is beyond measurement.

Facing Challenges

Being in a leadership position, you will inevitably face both large and small challenges. What you choose to do with those challenges will determine the type of leader you become.

For me, many of those challenges presented themselves in the form of feeling like I was not being heard. During my career as a high level executive in the banking industry, I can distinctly remember the feeling when I offered a suggestion to the regional managers of a large company while sitting around a table discussing a common problem. My suggestion was met with dead silence. For a moment, I wondered whether I had actually even spoken aloud.

Moments later, Jack, my male colleague, offered up an idea that sounded identical to mine. Everyone in the meeting jumped all over it, acknowledging his flash-of-lightning-like brilliance. "Hmmm. very interesting," I thought. "And frustrating." It felt like I was being completely ignored or as if I wasn't even in the room. Have *you* ever felt totally invisible?

While I chose not to react in the moment, I purposefully tucked that experience away as part of my learning process. For me, the lesson learned was that as a leader, you have to choose your battles carefully and exhibit grace under pressure, even if you are seething internally. Ultimately, many of those "filed" experiences contributed—in a meaningful and significant way—to the leader I chose to be. What experiences have *you* filed that have contributed to your growth as a leader?

On another occasion I was invited to attend the senior managers' meeting in Boston for the same company. I arrived excited to meet my peers from all around the Northeast. Several hundred attendees showed with only a small handful of them being female. I felt special! I was especially eager to meet the most senior women, believing it would be a great opportunity to compare notes. Imagine my surprise—and disappointment—to be brushed off in no uncertain terms by these very women!. Afterwards, a colleague told me that this happened because these women were fighting hard against the stereotype that they would hang together and not be able to "hold their own" with the men in the room. Ridiculous, I thought. But it was true.

Two important lessons: things aren't always what they seem to be and people do things for their own reasons, *not yours*.

In 2006, former Secretary of State Madeleine Albright said, "There's a special place in hell for women that don't help other women." I remember hearing these words at the time and reflecting on my own leadership journey in the workplace. Have you ever heard of the "queen bee syndrome"? Queen bees are women who actively work against other females in the workplace, impeding their path to success and equality, rather than offering encouragement or advice. I experienced it firsthand many times over.

> There's a special place in hell for women that don't help other women.
>
> —*Madeleine Albright*

When I was starting out as a young business leader, experiences like these were very common. This was a time in business when women didn't have mentors, networks or role models. Women were isolated islands. Mine was a sink-or-swim environment, and I was determined to learn to swim.

While the lack of support was often a disadvantage, there was an upside. It made me tough, resourceful, and very observant. I learned to choose my battles wisely. I understood the importance of getting results, and I realized that it was critically important to protect my reputation at all times. I created a clear line for myself that I would not cross.

To feed my rebellious streak, I wore bright colors instead of the required uniform: a navy, gray, or maroon suit with skirt (pants not allowed) plus a white shirt with a Peter Pan collar and a little floppy tie. I'm not making this up! It was hideous and reminiscent of the Catholic school uniform of my youth. I just couldn't do it, and decided that tastefully brightening up my business wardrobe was well worth the tradeoff of being me versus fitting in.

While it had been frustrating not to be taken seriously and even ignored, being underestimated provided me with a great opportunity to *observe quietly*—just as the proverbial fly on the wall. I learned a great deal about leadership this way. I learned what worked and what didn't work. And as I learned from others' mistakes, it was clear that most people were not paying attention. It allowed me to build a unique style and differentiate myself as a leader, which led to a lot of success and a lot of opportunity. There is always more than one vantage point to each situation.

This is how I came to believe that each and every experience you have can contribute to who you become as a leader. But this is only true if you have your ears perked up, your eyes wide open, and your attention focused!

When you pay attention, *you learn*. When you learn, *you grow*. And when you grow, *you create more opportunity*.

It is the challenges that make you stronger, more resilient, and savvier. They prepare you for the next level in your learning and development as a leader. Challenges ultimately prepare you to guide others through *their* learning curves. This is high-impact leadership at its best.

It is the challenges that make you stronger, more resilient, and savvier.

For me, it may have been because I was a female in a male-dominated world, or because my demeanor was more passive, or because I played the role that was slotted for me by my peers. Whatever the case may have been, the important point to remember is that the path to become an influential leader will not be paved with flat and level cement. In fact, it may feel more like a bumpy and dusty dirt road strewn with large rocks and surprising potholes. As you impart or continue on your leadership journey, remember that it will call for endurance, fortitude, and resilience. As you take the lessons in this book and build them into your everyday behavioral norms, you may still find obstacles that stand in your path, preventing your growth and transformation. Remember that these roads have been well-travelled by leaders before you. These challenges are an essential and inevitable part of the growing process.

Setting Your Own Agenda

As a leader, you need to create your own powerful, positive voice and set your own agenda. You will have negative experiences, which can lead to negative conditioning and an internal dialogue that is not supportive. People may say "you can't"; they may say "you're not good enough, not smart enough, not old enough, not young enough." If you are not careful, you might end up believing those voices. And then you will limit what you are capable of becoming.

Fortunately, I learned early on that I was underestimated, typically because of my gender. In the early days of the women's liberation movement, there was a great deal of resistance by both men *and women* to the idea that women should have equal rights under the law, be paid the same as men for the same jobs, and share in equal opportunity. Even today we are dealing with this problem. Catalyst.org indicates that the median annual earnings for full-time, year-round women workers in 2012 was $37,791 compared to men's $49,398. Furthermore, Forbes.

com reports that as of 2013, there were only 23 female CEOs of Fortune 500 companies.

Admittedly, like many young women of my generation, I was sent to college to meet a man who would support me and to "have something to fall back on." The problem for me was that I loved to learn and I also loved to work. After graduating from college, I got married, and even though I was adequately "taken care of," I chose to work. When looking for a job, I was told I was overqualified, lacked experience, and would be trained only to one day leave to have a baby. At the employment office, a caseworker inquired, "why don't you just go home and have babies like you're supposed to?" Upon being hired, I was challenged for accepting a job that should have gone to a man with a family to support. I was told that customers did not want to work with women. Looking back on it now, it seems unbelievable and rather humorous. But at the time it felt undeniably heartbreaking.

Based on an innate sense of fairness, I was an early feminist. This was another one of those choices I made based on my values, fully realizing this could hurt me "politically" in business. A colleague once told me I was smart and talented, but I was far too "strident" and I had to look up what that meant. Recently, I read that Brooksley Born, former chair of the Commodity Futures Trading Commission asked a good question "How many men are called *strident?*"

When you are determined to make a difference and to make a significant impact, not just "be successful," your motivation comes from a special place. When you are clear about your core values and what is important to you, you can make your decisions based on that knowledge and not based on someone else's idea of what you can or cannot be and should or should not do. This is what allows you to set your own agenda and find your own unique and authentic voice. Ultimately, when you shape your own path, and are guided by your own inner wisdom, you are able to operate with a clear conscience. People see this authenticity in you, and it becomes the basis of your personal power and strong leadership abilities.

Gaining Personal Power

You can learn a lot by watching how people with power use that power. And positional power is not as strong as personal power. The problem with relying on your position to lead is that it is not sustainable and it is not particularly effective. This type of leadership is based on rules, regulations, and a sense of entitlement. On the other hand, developing personal character, integrity, and trust travels with you wherever you go. Relationship-building skills are portable and transferable. That is a product of your journey, not your position. Positions transcend organizations, but strong leadership skills transcend time and place.

When I was building my business career, I often felt misunderstood, frustrated, and even invisible. I felt discouraged because I knew I had a lot to offer. I knew how hard I was willing to work, and I knew I could make a difference. I wanted to contribute—if only someone would give me a chance and believe in me.

> I never wanted to be the kind of leader that left people feeling the way I felt much of the time—underestimated, unappreciated, and underutilized.

What I chose to take away from those experiences was the certainty that I never wanted to be the kind of leader that left people feeling the way I felt much of the time—underestimated, unappreciated, and underutilized. As I was asked to take on greater leadership roles and responsibilities, I was determined to establish my own style, using my innate sense of fairness and balance. I was willing to challenge the status quo, fight for the underdogs and the disempowered, and take on the "sacred cows" of company culture. As a result, I was able to have made a significant impact and a meaningful difference. Together, you and I will work on your leadership approach to ensure you carry yourself with a strong voice, a precise vision, and a dedicated mission.

As a leader, you need to establish your own threshold for taking risk. Being clear about your personal values helps a great deal here. In retrospect, I took a lot of risks based on gut instinct, not by having a deliberate plan. Because of my optimistic nature, I usually saw more upside and less downside in the opportunities. Someone had to push the envelope—I thought, why not me? I discovered that people will stand behind someone who is out front, direct, and honest with them.

The willingness to take risk also contributes to your personal power. Courage is an interesting thing, and it's always relative. You aren't born with it; it's a choice. Generating the courage from within to take a stand, to make the unpopular decision, and to do the right thing when it's politically risky—are the very things that define you as a leader, contribute to your reputation, and build your personal power.

As I moved around the organization, I continued to establish myself as a different kind of leader. My line management experiences made me a better staff person, and my staff roles made me a better line manager. I also developed a strong network across the organization through my experiences working in many locations and many different business units. As the organization got larger and more complex, these relationships were advantageous because it became more difficult to find people willing to collaborate to get things done. This is how I learned about the importance of personal power.

Building your personal power will take you much further than any title or credentials. Your ability to connect with and influence people comes from decisions, actions, and behaviors that demonstrate your core values. Your journey will project your character. The degree to which you act, decide, and behave in ways consistent and congruent with what you say is important will define your reputation. It will also determine your overall impact as a leader, so you better be clear about your intention.

Have you ever noticed how often there's a big difference between the way we see ourselves and the way others—especially our team members—see us?

It's so easy to assume that other people see the same things we see. So many leaders do this, and it leads to misunderstanding, lack of alignment, and suboptimal results. Closing the gap between the leader you want to be and the leader you are perceived to be can really increase your leadership effectiveness dramatically. Throughout this book, we will work hard to ensure you are projecting your goals and your character as a leader. It does not happen overnight. But through conscious leadership decisions and positive behavioral traits, it will happen. I can promise you that.

> Learning to recognize and develop your strengths and the strengths of others is a far better focus for your leadership than trying to "fix" what's broken in people.

Leading with Strengths

For leaders, the journey to projecting a positive mission and vision starts with leading with your strengths. Learning to recognize and develop your strengths and the strengths of others is a far better focus for your leadership than trying to "fix" what's broken in people.

During a routine performance review, my manager pointed out: "Cheryl, your biggest problem is that you always see the best in people— and situations. You are not critical enough. You need to focus more attention on people's weaknesses and help them to improve in those areas, or you will never be successful here."

"Wow!" I thought, "I'd better fix that!" So I set out to identify what was wrong with people and to help them correct their deficiencies. But there were two problems with that: 1) It was hard for me to see what was wrong. 2) It was even harder for me to have the conversation with any conviction. In other words, it did not feel authentic. Doing this did not fit with who I was. And it's hard to be something you're not and do it convincingly. People see through it.

Then I read two marvelous books by the brilliant Marcus Buckingham: *First, Break All the Rules* and *Now, Discover Your Strengths*. The premise of these books is that working to leverage and develop your strengths is far more beneficial and effective than trying to address your weaknesses. It felt as if those books were written for me. Reading them saved my concept of what good leadership should be.

Using Buckingham's philosophy, my leadership team was able to create incredible synergy by allowing people to focus their time, energy, and attention on things they excelled at and enjoyed, while minimizing the time they spent on things outside their strength zones. What a concept!

The lesson: learn to focus on strengths. And it's another indication that by following your own instincts, your own inner voice will most likely serve you better than taking advice from someone with a very different philosophy about people and leadership.

This does not mean ignoring your blind spots or weaknesses; on the contrary, know what those are and work to minimize any negative impact they may have. Ignoring your weaknesses or trying to hide them is foolish because the thing about blind spots is this: *everyone else can see them except you!* Acknowledging them will contribute to greater authenticity, greater credibility, and ultimately greater effectiveness for you and everyone on your team.

> Acknowledging your blind spots will contribute to great authenticity, greater credibility, and ultimately greater effectiveness for you and everyone on your team.

Recently, one of my mentors gave the members of our mastermind group an assignment: Thinking about the successes you've had in your life, what are the five recurring themes? In other words, what traits have contributed to your success time and time again?

Within a few minutes, I quickly identified:

1. My love of learning new things and desire for continuous improvement
2. My optimistic attitude
3. My perspective; i.e., not sweating the small stuff
4. My interest in connecting and collaborating with others
5. My drive and perseverance

Additionally, my sense of humor and a sense of adventure and passion for making a difference have absolutely contributed to the leader I've become.

Do this activity for yourself and ask your team members to do it as well. Then, whenever you face challenges, look at the list and ask yourself which of those attributes you need to bring into play. Ask yourself what's missing in the moment that has helped you succeed in the past. This seemingly minor activity will help you overcome major challenges.

My Strengths

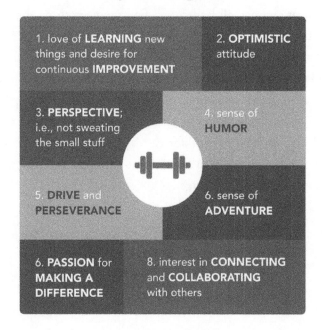

1. love of **LEARNING** new things and desire for continuous **IMPROVEMENT**

2. **OPTIMISTIC** attitude

3. **PERSPECTIVE**; i.e., not sweating the small stuff

4. sense of **HUMOR**

5. **DRIVE** and **PERSEVERANCE**

6. sense of **ADVENTURE**

6. **PASSION** for **MAKING A DIFFERENCE**

8. interest in **CONNECTING** and **COLLABORATING** with others

Beyond that, use the list as a guide to keeping your focus and attention on what is special and unique about you. Resolve to bring more of that into your daily work and daily life as it will make you an ever better role model for others.

Turning challenges into learning opportunities, setting your own agenda, finding your own voice, developing your personal power, and using the wisdom gained from your successes are all important contributors to your leadership.

> We don't receive wisdom; we must discover it for ourselves after a journey that no one can take for us or spare us.
>
> *– Marcel Proust*

Marcel Proust said, "We don't receive wisdom; we must discover it for ourselves after a journey that no one can take for us or spare us." At one point or another, all leaders will find the need to put one foot in front of the other and begin the journey. For some, those first few steps are the most difficult part. It becomes easier as momentum builds. But inevitably the obstacles will present themselves. They may be small rocks creating an unsteady road, or large boulders blocking your path. For me it was the struggle of finding an identity and a voice in a very male-oriented and dominated workforce. My journey eventually sculpted who I am today and allowed me to break through the limiting beliefs and overcome difficult challenges.

> One who gains strength by overcoming obstacles possesses the only strength which can overcome adversity.
> – *Albert Schweitzer*

Albert Schweitzer said, "One who gains strength by overcoming obstacles possesses the only strength which can overcome adversity." Your journey will not only define and mold your abilities, it will push you to become stronger than you were when you began your travels. Overcoming obstacles strengthens your heart and soul and allows you to manage and surmount even bigger future challenges. Embrace the journey and recognize it may not always be a sweat-free and mentally comfortable experience. In the end you will find yourself to be a stronger leader, with a sound vision, and the ability to inspire and motivate others to begin their own journeys. As we move forward, embrace the growth, get excited for the journey, and make the most of the obstacles. Ultimately, it's your choice to do so.

☞ Usable Insights

- Recognize the value of the struggles, obstacles and difficult choices in your learning and development process.
- When you pay attention, you learn. When you learn, you grow. And when you grow, you create more opportunity. It is the challenges that make you stronger, more resilient and savvier.
- Learn by watching how people use their power and recognize the difference between positional and personal power. Create your own powerful, positive voice and set your own agenda.
- Focus on recognizing and developing your strengths and those of others instead of "fixing" what's broken.

Action Steps

1. Identify and list 5 of the key strengths that you have used to gain success in the past.
2. Identify a current challenge or obstacle you are currently facing and determine which of those strengths can be applied in providing a solution.

Chapter 3

From Position to Influence:
Leading Without a Title

Leadership is influence; nothing more, nothing less.
—John Maxwell

As you travel through the trials and tribulations of building strong leadership traits, you will find the journey to be one that is both challenging and enormously exciting. Those with whom you surround yourself can aid in this journey. They are the elevators, the motivators, and the people that breathe life into your voyage. Far too often, people take the journey without evaluating and analyzing the leaders who came before them. When you think about the people *you* most admire as leaders, what do they have in common?

What is it that causes you to connect with them? And how is it that they influence you?

During leadership workshops, I often ask attendees to consider the great, effective leaders they have known or observed in their lives—they may be government or political leaders, religious or community leaders, business leaders, or maybe someone for whom they have worked. I ask, "What were some of the qualities that made them great leaders?" And then I have attendees call out the words and phrases that define leadership.

Whenever I do this activity, I'm always struck by just how much we expect from our leaders. Understandably, there's always a long list of what we expect to see in leadership.

The other thing that's notable and consistent about the list of leadership attributes is that, while it's true that some people seem to be "born leaders," most of these qualities involve the choices we make on the inside of our lives.

> Everyone has the ability and potential for success as a leader.

What's really exciting is that these choices can be taught and they can be learned. *Everyone has the ability and potential for success as a leader.* Together we will focus on this essential message.

So how do you go about developing those traits in yourself that you most admire in others? How do you use those traits to better connect with others? And how does this all lead to increasing your level of influence with others?

The Leader of Yesterday vs. the Leader of Tomorrow

Since effective leadership in the twenty-first century is about developing the ability to connect with others and influence them, let's draw the distinction between positional leadership and influential leadership:

POSITIONAL LEADER	INFLUENTIAL LEADER
Relies on title, credentials, rights; operates with sense of entitlement, uses fear and intimidation to direct others.	Relies on the ability to connect with and influence others; builds relationships and trust; uses encouragement to help others succeed.
Uses power to force his or her way; not open to other points of view or challenge.	Shares power, responsibility, and accountability to accomplish goals.
Focused on self-promotion and forward progress; reputation.	Takes responsibility for what goes wrong; gives credit for what goes right.
Focused on results and takes credit for successes; quick to blame others or make excuses for failures.	Values different backgrounds, experiences, cultures; seeks ideas and opinions from a wide range of perspectives.
Values personal knowledge, skills, and abilities more than other people; not open to feedback, questions—"my way or the highway."	Focuses on developing other leaders, sharing opportunities for growth and development.
Only knows one way to lead—and isn't interested in changing or adapting.	Understands how (and is able) to lead from the front and from the back.

The Positional Leader

The positional leader relies on his title and position to accomplish results. He believes that people working "under" him should do things his way because he is the boss and knows best. When questioned about the reasons or wisdom of a particular course of action, he thinks *because I said so!*

A positional leader implements a "my way or the highway" philosophy to enforce his will, believing that his position gives him (as a matter of right) the power to act in the way he believes to be best. After all, didn't the powers-that-be confer that status on him because of his knowledge, skills, and abilities? As a result, he is confident in that and does not see any reason to adapt or change his approach.

Very often the positional leader will view questions or challenges as a test of wills. He lacks any patience or tolerance for it. He may even lash out in anger, throwing things, slamming things, shouting, and even cursing when he doesn't get his way right away.

I once worked for such a man. Let's call him Bob. Bob was a bully and famous for his temper tantrums. One day I walked into his office for our regularly scheduled update meeting. At the time, I was running a large complex project for him. Without warning, he started in on me, ranting and raving about anything and everything for what seemed like forever. When he paused, I looked him straight in the eye and asked if he felt better now. Then I told him that while I was sure I deserved that outburst, I had no clue why and maybe he could enlighten me so that I could avoid such future behavior. And then I asked if we could continue as two mature adults to discuss whatever needed to be discussed.

Despite his behavior, Bob had achieved a very high level of responsibility in the organization. Fear and intimidation were his methods of choice to drive results. He didn't see any reason to change since it had worked so well for him to this point. Today, I don't think it would be tolerated. It certainly would not be effective. It didn't work for me, and I chose to stand up to it because I decided the risk of consequences outweighed this immature behavior.

Working for Bob was not one of the highlights of my career. But the lesson I want to share is that you always have at least two choices (sometimes more) in the way you respond to situations. You also have a choice in how to behave in the first place and how you will respond to disappointment or mistakes or failures. You can choose the type of leader you want to be and behave in a way consistent with that type of leader. And you can choose to adapt to changing times, different needs, and different cultures and styles. Your level of influence with people expands when you do this effectively.

The Influential Leader

The influential leader is concerned with building relationships and trust. She knows that in order to succeed, she needs to rely on the support of others. This requires connecting the team with her vision, missions, and values and then aligning the team in support of her direction. However, along the journey she is not only open to the questions, feedback, and insights from others, but she actually seeks out a wide range of perspectives as a way to broaden her own. She values and respects those with different experiences who see things from different angles and willingly shares the spotlight with her team. She does not hoard power but distributes it, encouraging participation and full engagement.

The most effective leaders learn how to share credit for successes and take full responsibility for failures, recognizing that every failure is an opportunity to learn and grow within their organizations. Therefore, they encourage risk-taking and focus their attention on the development of other leaders, looking for opportunities to expose them to experiences that will challenge, stretch, and take them beyond their current capabilities.

In contrast, positional leaders will focus solely on their own successes, taking full credit for them, seeking full recognition and forward motion with greater responsibility. They are quick to deflect blame onto others and have ready-prepared excuses and reasons for failed opportunities. Since they only know one way to lead, they treat performers and non-performers alike; if they are focused on the potential in others, it is only for purposes of making themselves look good.

> The influential leader knows how to lead from the front, from behind and even sideways.

The influential leader knows how to lead from the front, from behind, and even sideways. She is tuned in to the needs of others and to their unique strengths and abilities to contribute. She organizes the team in such a way to get the most out of each person's talents while minimizing the impact of their weaknesses and blind spots. Remember that leaders are like elevators: they can take you to great heights or down to low depths. But ultimately it is your decision which directional button you push and whether you get on or not.

Learning to Lead from Within™

The framework discussed here is designed to help you make the transformation from a positional leader—where we all start—to a leader with the ability to connect with others and influence them. As I describe the elements in this framework, you will see the extent to which positional leaders don't consider these elements of effective leadership. Neither are they particularly interested in developing them. And you will also see how your development into an influential leader depends on mastering this process, starting with your mindset and thought process.

Four of the components to the *Learning to Lead from Within* framework are:

1. Culture
2. Clarity
3. Connection
4. Clout

Learning to Lead from Within is centered on the goal of forming an endless loop, representing the continuous learning, growth, and improvement process that represents leadership development. The glue that holds it all together is *commitment.* Commitment is at the center of this loop because it needs to be ever-present, and it relates to each of the other components at all times. Without commitment, there is little progress and little growth. And when the going gets tough, which it will, it's your level of commitment that provides the resolve to keep moving forward.

Learning Lead from Within™ Framework

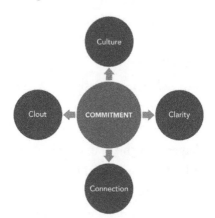

Understanding the Big Picture

Let's break down the elements of *Learning to Lead from Within* to ensure you have a strong understanding of each of its respective parts. The starting point of this framework is your **internal culture** — or your personal psychology. This includes how you think, how you feel, and how you behave. It's about your DNA. It's about understanding what drives you and what makes you *uniquely* you. It's about how you choose and create your reality. Mastering your internal culture forms the foundation of learning to lead from the inside out.

What does it mean to master your internal culture? It means learning to be deliberate about how you think, how you feel, and how you act. In order to do that, you need to be more aware of your thoughts and feelings. In fact, you need to choose them. Recognizing the power of your thoughts is crucial to your success.

Clarity

The next element in the framework is **clarity**: understanding who you are, what you stand for, and why you are here. For a positional leader, this is just about exerting the power that comes with the title or position. But to become influential, clarity needs to include deliberate thought and action about what you want and don't want—in all aspects of your life. It's about what you want to do, who you want to be, and what you want to have.

> Clarity allows you to focus your attention, your energy, and your time.

Clarity allows you to focus your attention, your energy, and your time. Clarity enables you to live on purpose and make choices that are intentional and consistent with the leader you want to become. Clarity allows you to see clearly through the fog.

For example, when you start with the end in mind, it's so much easier to make the decisions that will enable accomplishing the goal. When you know the destination and have a vision for what you want to achieve, it allows you to take inspired action and be alert to resources and opportunities that will support your efforts.

In later chapters, you will work on gaining *clarity of thinking*. And you will meet some of the people who demonstrate just how clarity of thinking leads to more effective, more influential leadership.

Connection

The next element, **connection**, has two aspects. The first is about the connection you have with yourself as you gain clarity. It's what allows you to behave in alignment with your core values and beliefs. And it represents consistency and transparency to those around you. This is especially important in leadership because you will create confusion and ambiguity if you are not congruent between what you say and what you do. Your message will not be clear.

> Leadership is much less about what you do, and much more about who you are.
>
> *—Frances Hesselbein*

Ultimately, people follow the greatest leaders because of who they are and what they represent. When you think about the outstanding leaders in your own experience and observation, this is often what causes you to connect with them and be influenced by them. Martin Luther King Jr. stood for racial equality and peaceful protest. He learned these methods from Gandhi, who focused on making life better for all people in the world. Then there is Nelson Mandela, whose message stood to end poverty and inequality across the world. These leaders moved mountains. And they did so through their ability to influence and invigorate others through their purposeful messages.

Connection is also about how you interact with others. Your abilities to establish creditability, develop relationships, and build trust are the essential elements of creating connections with others.

Clout

Connection ultimately leads to the final element in the framework: the opportunity to influence others through your level of **clout**. It's difficult to create the kinds of connections that enable your ability to influence and lead others unless you've done the inside work of mastering your psychology and gaining clarity of purpose.

> Influence is the currency of leadership.

Influence is the currency of leadership. Leaders trade in influence the way brokers buy and sell stocks. The ability to persuade followers to align with your vision, support your goals and objectives, and execute according to your plan is essential to the role of leadership. And your ability to influence others will ultimately determine your success as a leader.

This all leads us to the glue—commitment. Everything rises and falls with *commitment*, the central element in the framework. You first become aware of the need to improve, planting the seed and desire to change. When you hit the inevitable roadblocks, it is your commitment that sustains you throughout the journey. These same commitments also propel you to higher levels and greater successes.

Commitment will drive you to cultivate in yourself the *attitudes* that differentiate leaders from others, the essential *behaviors* that leaders need to consistently model, the *competencies* that make leaders effective and the *perspectives* that leaders need to develop and maintain.

In this book we are exploring the *thinking* part of your personal psychology. The thinking part is the most essential part, yet it's the part people often fail to consider. People think all the time; they just don't think the right things.

Reaping the Rewards

Most people don't *think* about leadership at all. If they do, they think about it as a title or as a position. Most people don't consider what it takes to be a good leader. Even folks in leadership positions rarely sit down and evaluate their duties and responsibilities as leaders. Thus, most people don't bother to ask: how do I improve *my* ability as a leader?

And when most people *do* decide to improve as a leader, they want to know "what do I have to *do*" differently? And it's certainly important to learn how to *do* things differently.

It's important to learn and develop new skills, to know your own strengths, to then recognize strengths in others, and finally to identify your blind spots or those things that get in your way and put an abrupt halt to growth.

It's also important to communicate with clarity, to delegate effectively, to set vision, to gain alignment, and to provide direction and feedback. There's an endless list of leadership skills, knowledge, and abilities to learn about and then develop. No wonder leadership development is a lifelong pursuit!

So many business leaders are so busy *doing* that they take for granted the need for *being* and the need for *thinking*. They actually neglect to take time to think strategically.

Learning to *think differently* as a leader, to take control of your thinking, and to be deliberate and intentional about it will enable you to become the influential leader you are capable of being. It will enable you to maximize your ability to connect and your ability to influence. Thinking differently will lead to bigger and better results.

> "We cannot solve our problems with the same level of *thinking* that created them."
>
> – *Albert Einstein*

After all, as Albert Einstein told us: "We cannot solve our problems with the same level of *thinking* that created them."

As a leader, your level of thinking is critical. Your mindset is far more important than your skill set. *How you think and how you influence others to think are the most essential leadership skills of all.*

We all struggle with fears and doubts and limiting beliefs. We all struggle with negative thinking that doesn't serve our best interests. In the past, I've been the victim of such negative thinking myself. I'd be willing to guess that at some point you were as well.

Here's the lesson: unless you learn how to manage your thinking, your thinking will end up managing you. Unless you learn to quiet the negative voices—to overcome the doubts and questions and dispel the limiting beliefs—you will remain closer to the positional leader end of the spectrum. You will struggle with your ability to connect, build strong relationships, create and sustain trust, and apply influence.

Your thinking forms the very *foundation* of your leadership. Without a solid foundation, there is nothing to build on. There is nowhere to go and no way to grow. However, learning to think like an influential leader will give you a strong foundation and a solid base. Once you learn how to think like an influential leader, things will never be the same and you will never be the same.

Bridging the Gap

Here are some of the ways that developing your thinking will improve your leadership ability and credibility and move you in the direction of a greater influence:

1. ***You will learn how to quiet the negative voices in your head.*** This can be very powerful in maintaining a positive attitude and demonstrating the level of confidence people expect from you as a leader. Learning to take control of your thoughts will make a big difference in your level of influence. In chapter 9 you will meet Jackie, who experienced the power of turning her negative voices away in favor of positive, empowering ones, adding to her own strength of character and her potential to lead others. Most people have negative voices and yet they don't realize they have a choice about whether or not to listen. You do have a choice. You too will learn how to exercise that choice.

2. ***You will be better equipped to overcome your fears.*** We all have fears. When you know how to put your worries and

hesitations into their appropriate place, in proper perspective, you can act with more *courage*, enabling you to make longer strides much more quickly. Followers admire courage. I love the stories of these "famous failures" who had to overcome fears or negative feedback from others and move forward toward their greatness:

- The aspiring high school basketball player who was cut from the team, went home, locked himself in his room, and cried. We came to know him as Michael Jordan, perhaps the greatest basketball player ever.

- The woman demoted from her job as a news anchor because she "wasn't fit for television." Yes, Oprah Winfrey went on to become one of the most powerful forces in the history of TV.

- Decca Recording Studios rejected the group and said "We don't like their sound" and "They have no future in show business." Who was that group? The Beatles.

Don't you wonder what would have happened if these leaders gave in to *their* fears or to the negative noise surrounding their goals? How would you benefit by having some of their courage for moving past your fears?

3. ***You will be more prepared for leadership opportunities that come your way.*** You will learn to recognize those opportunities, and you will know what to do with them when they show up. How many times in your life or professional career or your business have you looked back with regret because of a missed opportunity? You will be in a better position to take advantage of leadership opportunities when you learn *how* and *why* to think as a leader. It's amazing the difference this can make when you've given thought to how you want to be perceived as a leader; you

actually see things that were always there and you just weren't paying attention.

After reading Ken Blanchard's book *The One Minute Manager*, we tested a campaign of our own to "catch people doing something right" within our organization. This one small change completely transformed the entire atmosphere of that workplace. Everyone began to look for opportunities to recognize their coworkers, to appreciate each other, and to help each other. It was powerful and lasting. And it was all because we trained ourselves to *think* differently, to look for the opportunities—not the problems—that were always right there in front of us.

4. ***You will improve your ability to focus your attention, energy, and time to get bigger and better results.*** And, in turn, you will be in a better position to help others to do the same. Thinking leads to clarity. Clarity allows you to focus. Ultimately, when you are clear you spend less time and energy to accomplish more things. You pay more attention to what's important and what serves your purpose. And you are better positioned to fend off the inevitable distractions.

You can create a shorter distance between where you are and where you want to be. It's like setting the destination on your personal GPS system. Once the destination is set, the roadmap is clear. And so are the incremental steps that you need to take. All you need to do is follow them.

The Likely Result

Developing your thinking will improve your leadership ability, and your increased credibility will ultimately allow you to be more influential. As a result, you will be able to make a bigger difference and have a greater impact on your team and the success of your business.

Everything improves when you grow as a leader. Your life improves and so does your business. Even your outlook improves along with your results. You can impact not only your own life but also the lives of people around you—your family, your coworkers, your team, your entire organization, your community, and maybe even the world. There really is no limit to the potential for greater leadership and greater influence.

There has never been a greater need for leadership than there is right now. The world is moving faster and faster. The speed of life is lapping the speed of light. Things are changing all around us. As a leader, you have access to more information. You have more choices and more decisions to make. You are the beacon of hope and the executor of solutions.

When it comes to leading others, you have more responsibility too. People are looking to you to show the way. You are the modern-day lighthouse guiding the ships to safe travels. And it's important to do that deliberately and with intention. It's important to do that on purpose. With purpose, vision is achieved. Success is obtained. People are happy.

> Being a more influential leader all starts with you learning to lead you. Your biggest leadership challenge is your biggest leadership opportunity.

Being a more influential leader all starts with you learning to lead you. Your biggest leadership challenge is your biggest leadership opportunity. It all starts with doing the tough inside work. It starts with managing your personal psychology: how you think, how you feel, and how you behave.

The transformation that you will experience and inspire others to experience will not only be personally rewarding, but it will also position you to lead well into the future, as the requirements continue to shift and the pace escalates. The transformation from positional leader to influential leader is the difference between moving rocks and moving mountains; the difference between changing results and changing lives— the ability to change a person, not just an idea. It is what separates the winners from the losers, the real from the fake, the meaningful from the meaningless. But ultimately it is what the Gandhis and Martin Luther King Jr.s and Nelson Mandelas used to change the world.

☞ Usable Insights

- There is a clear distinction between the leaders of yesterday, who relied primarily on their positions, and the leaders of tomorrow, who rely on the ability to connect with and influence others.
- The Learning to Lead from Within™ framework provides a continuous loop of development that includes mastering your internal **culture**, and recognizing the need for **clarity** to create the level of **connection** that leads to influential **clout**. Your level of **commitment** drives your forward movement, learning and growth.
- Learning to manage your thoughts will
  - ○ Improve your leadership ability, credibility and influence,
  - ○ Help you overcome fears and doubts,
  - ○ Enable you to focus your time, energy and attention and
  - ○ Lead to greater opportunity.

🐾 Actions Steps

1. Think of a leader you know that uses influential power instead of positional power. What is she doing that reflects her use of influence and how can you apply it to your leadership?
2. What words would you use to describe your ideal internal culture – how you think, how you feel, how you behave?

Chapter 4

We Are All Game Changers:
Evaluating Your Leadership Type

*If you're waiting for someone to save you, to save your company,
your community or to save the world—they're not coming. It's up
to us—you and me.*

—Bo Eason

Here's a little realized truth: anyone can be a leader. When we think about leaders, we often think of those people who have made a major historical splash. Men like Abraham Lincoln, Martin Luther King Jr., and Nelson Mandela. Women like Oprah Winfrey, Angela Merkel, and Melinda Gates. There are leaders in government, religion, business, philanthropy, and the arts.

Leadership is not about position or title or how many people answer to you. In reality, it's about your ability to connect with others and influence people. Thus, we all have the ability to lead. Some lead deliberately and others simply rise to the occasion when the moment presents itself. Some leaders are global in their influence; others may impact only a few in their lifetime. No matter how many or why, leaders come in many different shapes and sizes. Leaders exhibit different styles and have different personal traits; they travel different paths.

Through my journey I have identified five different categories of leaders, each with their own set of qualities and characteristics, but all impactful and influential enough to be called leaders:

1. Trailblazers: those who pave the way for others by daring to challenge the status quo in spite of disapproval, criticism, and even personal danger.
2. Role Models: those who provide an example through deliberate and consistent thoughts, words, and actions.
3. Visionary Leaders: those who see clearly into the future, have a steadfast belief in what's possible, and take the necessary risks to achieve it.
4. Servant Leaders: those who are focused on others with respect, value, and belief; they inspire the best in others and are focused on their success.
5. Transformational Leaders: those driven by a belief, a cause, or a purpose that is much bigger than themselves as they courageously seek to create a sustainable change in thinking or behavior.

Trailblazers

According to *New York Times* editorial columnist Gail Collins, "Gloria Steinem occupies a singular place in American culture. In the 1960s and 1970s the whole concept of a woman's place was transformed—discrimination was outlawed, hearts and minds were opened. In the history of our gender, this might have been the grandest moment. There were all kinds of reasons that the change happened at that particular time, and a raft of female leaders who pushed the movement along. But when people think about it, Gloria Steinem is the first name that pops up. She's the face of feminism."

Gloria Steinem is a trailblazer. As a journalist and political social activist, she became the voice of the feminist movement and a hero to a generation of women who were frustrated with having to make a choice between a career and a family. She was a co-founder of the feminist-themed *Ms.* magazine as well as multiple organizations dedicated to securing civil rights for women and minorities. Writing passionately about the benefits of equality, and testifying before the Senate hearings, Steinem was perhaps the most vocal, active campaigner for the Equal Rights Amendment. Today, at age eighty, she continues to write and speak out as the most prominent radical feminist of our time.

Trailblazers dare to go where no one has dared before. They pave the way. They usually have strong feelings, opinions, or beliefs that drive their actions. They are often willing to take great risks in the name of their causes and usually describe those difficult decisions as something they just "had to do." They can find themselves subjected to enormous ridicule, criticism, and even physical danger as they move in the direction of their goal or purpose. But they make it safer for those who come next.

Kathy Switzer is a trailblazer too. She is an author, TV commentator, and avid runner best known for breaking the gender barrier in marathon running. In 1967 she entered the Boston Marathon using her initials, K.V. Switzer, and received her number, 261. Running with her boyfriend and her trainer, she was suddenly attacked by the race organizer, who grabbed her and yelled for her to "get the hell out of my race and give me those numbers." It was all captured on film and broadcast worldwide, resulting in a ban on women from all competition with male runners.

Although she and other runners tried to convince the race organizers to change this rule, it wasn't until 1972 that women were welcome to the Boston Marathon. Switzer was the women's winner in the 1974 New York Marathon. *Runner's World* magazine named her Female Runner of the Decade. Her memoir, *Marathon Woman*—published on the fortieth anniversary of her history-making run—won the Billie Award for journalism for its inspiring portrayal of women in sports. In 2011 Switzer was inducted into the National Women's Hall of Fame for "creating a social revolution by empowering women all around the world through running." She continues to compete and to improve opportunities for women runners in different parts of the world.

Karen Martinez is a trailblazer as well. Having started her industry-leading business in 1997 with one employee and her first contract, she has grown Bravo! Building Services to one of the largest privately held facility and outsourcing companies in the country. With over 3,400 team members servicing more than 50 million square feet along the US Eastern Seaboard, Bravo! provides a full range of expert services including janitorial, mechanical engineering, and HVAC service/repair.

Her motto is simple: "Do what you say you are going to do." In an industry with typically high turnover, Karen's company experiences only 6 percent employee turnover and retains an impressive 98.8 percent of its customers. She has grown the company through strategic acquisitions and added capability and certifications that put the company on the leading edge of the industry. She was honored as Entrepreneur of the Year by Ernst & Young and Distinguished Citizen of the Year by the Boy Scouts of America. And Bravo! has been consistently named one of the top woman-owned businesses, top diversity-owned businesses, and top small businesses in the United States.

Amna Al Haddad is a successful competitive weightlifter. Despite misconceptions and even heavy criticism, she is making an impact by pursuing her passion while pushing against the societal norms of her country. She is a Muslim from the United Arab Emirates and the first woman to compete. Amna has made a choice to do what's right for her instead of what others believe is right. She is willing and able to overcome the obstacles of her choice. And, as a journalist, she understands the responsibility that comes with representing both your country and your religion to the world.

These trailblazers are driven by something inside that guides their actions and their conviction. Sometimes they are trying to prove they are up to the task; sometimes they want to prove that others are, despite conventional wisdom or stereotypes. Through their leadership, they create a new paradigm of what's possible.

At the end of the day, trailblazers:

- are driven by their passion and inner voice
- take risks and work persistently toward the outcome they want to achieve
- demonstrate great courage in the face of challenges
- create a new reality and perception of what's possible

Role Models

Whether they realize it or not, all leaders are role models. That includes parents. Have you ever witnessed a two-year-old blurt out something her parents wish she hadn't? Usually it's something she heard from them! Children learn very early to follow the leader. And as we grow up we are often unconscious of the degree to which we look to others for our own cues on how to behave and what to say.

The best leaders know this and work hard to ensure that their behaviors and their words are congruent. Perhaps the best model of this was Mahatma Gandhi. You may have heard the story of the mother who traveled for days to ask the great leader to tell her son, a diabetic, to stop consuming sugar. She was sent away and told to return in three weeks' time, simply because Gandhi would not instruct the young boy to give up sugar while he himself consumed it. He always sought for equanimity of his thoughts, feelings, words, and actions; it seems an apt definition of integrity.

When leaders are deliberate about modeling the behavior they want to see in the world, they are simultaneously thinking about the long-term consequences of their actions. They are working to develop themselves from the inside out because they realize that is the best path to congruence.

Role models operate in accordance with their core values, and they form good habits and are disciplined about them. They are focused on the outcome and clear about their priorities. They know that in the process of empowering others, their actions speak so much louder than their words.

Bo Eason made it a policy to be the first to show up on the practice field and the last to leave. He just knew that in order to be the best, he had to work harder and longer than anyone else. That may have been a product of always being told he was too slow, too small, and too weak to play pro football.

When he was traded to the San Francisco Forty-Niners after four years with the Houston Oilers, he arrived at training camp and headed out to practice about an hour ahead of time, as usual. But someone was already there. It was Jerry Rice.

The receivers lined up, and one at a time they trotted out, made their half spin to catch the passes thrown by Joe Montana, then stopped and walked over to hand the football back to Joe. The ritual was repeated, receiver after receiver.

Then it was Jerry Rice's turn. He dashed off at full speed, turned, caught the pass, and continued at full speed to the other end of the field, then turned and ran back at full speed to hand the ball to Joe.

Later, in the locker room, Bo asked Jerry why he was always moving at full speed. After all, Jerry Rice was already the best wide receiver in the history of the sport. "Easy," said Jerry. "When these hands touch the ball, this body winds up in the end zone." He practiced that sequence again and again and again, and then repeated it in the game more than anyone else before him or since.

No one ever worked harder at the game than Jerry Rice, and his intensive training was an inspiration to all the other players. With a work ethic like that, is it any wonder that Rice's 1,549 career receptions are 307 receptions ahead of second place, or that his 22,895 receiving yards are 6,961 ahead of the next closest receiver? In Jerry Rice's 20 seasons in the NFL, he missed only 10 games, and his 303 games are by far the most of any wide receiver in history.

Bo considers Jerry the most generous of pros. Generosity, to Bo, is the art of giving all of yourself all the time. He describes Jerry as having a very big influence on his life. I would add that Bo brings that same level of generosity to his clients as a trainer and coach for people who want to be the absolute best onstage.

Bo is currently in his third career. After pro football, he studied with the best of the best to become a stage actor, then wrote, directed, and produced his own one-man play about his life, *The Runt of the Litter*, in which he plays himself, his more-famous brother, his father, his mother, and his coaches—all with astonishing credibility. It is a powerful story and the most unforgettable, physically intense performance I have ever seen.

And now Bo Eason trains other public speakers who want to present themselves and their stories powerfully onstage. He works only with those who are determined to be the best. He gives generously of his talent and experience—he continues to be "all in" and to play "all out."

As a leader, you must always be asking yourself the question: Who can I serve? What more can I give? How can I do better and be better so that those who follow learn and grow and improve? It is the role of the role model, and all leaders are role models, whether they are conscious and intentional about it or not. But some do the talking while others do the marching. And that is what truly creates the most impactful role models around. You need to ask yourself what kind of behavior, attitude, and mindset you are modeling for those who follow. And are you deliberately choosing that behavior, attitude, and mindset?

At the end of the day, role models are those who:

- are aware of the impact of their actions
- strive toward continuous improvement
- seek to be congruent in thoughts, words, and actions
- provide an example to others

Visionary Leaders

Visionary leaders are those who can see clearly into the future. They are strategic in their focus. Their willingness and ability to take risks is fueled by their clear view of the destination. And they know that to execute effectively they need to communicate with clarity about the desired outcome and the direction, as well as the boundaries within which to operate.

The best leaders are able to use their influence to build alignment around their vision and create momentum toward it. They have an internal locus of control, and they will take the initiative and make decisions that generate forward motion. When confronted with obstacles, they will either go straight through or over them, work around them, or turn the challenge into an opportunity. They are fixed on the long-term view.

Joey Reiman has been called the "Moses of Marketing" and cited by FastCompany as one of the people who will change the way we live and work. He is an adjunct professor at Emory University's Goizueta Business School, where his course on Ideation has "changed the way business leaders and students view the power of thinking to create success through social good." He is founder and CEO of Bright House, The Ideation Corporation*, which is "known for its work in the areas of ideation, purpose-inspired leadership, innovation, and marketing." Working with clients that include such well-known brands as Coca-Cola, McDonald's, Proctor & Gamble, and Newell Rubbermaid, he has helped them to transform by moving beyond wealth creation and shareholder value, uncovering their purpose or "soulful excellence," and becoming both a financial and humanitarian force for good.

Joey Reiman is a visionary thought leader in the world of business. His formula to transform business, described in his book *The Story of Purpose: The Path to Creating a Brighter Brand, a Greater Company, and a Lasting Legacy,* is not only powerful and inspirational but also proven and time-tested. He proposes a different model for measuring success in business that moves beyond profits and stock prices to embrace contribution and impact— and create a so-called "Purpose 500" of companies that are doing well by doing good.

Joey advocates moving "from a brand to a stand" and believes that "when purpose leads, profit follows." He describes purpose-inspired leaders as those who have the ability to transform their associates, their companies, and even the world by creating a culture centered on *meaning* and making the world a better place. He offers a framework to bring this concept to life in an organization with the articulation of a "master idea," which becomes the battle cry that provides marching orders for the team.

One way Joey brings this concept to life in his own organization is through the observation of March Fourth Day, a day for the entire team to take on their own pursuit of purpose in their lives in whatever way they deem fit. On March 4 of each calendar year, Joey gives his fifty-plus team members the day off so they can take steps or even strides toward their own dreams.

In the epilogue to his book, he mentions that March 4 is also the day in 1957 that marks the introduction of the S&P stock market index, the standard of business financial success, while he proposes its new measure: purpose. And he points out that purpose-driven companies outperform S&P 500 companies by over 1000 percent. (Sisodia, Wolfe, and Sheth, *Firms of Endearment*)

I have spoken often about the need to bring more humanity to leadership; in other words, more of a desire to serve than to be served. Joey takes this a giant step forward by proposing that businesses bring *more humanity* and *more meaning* into the workplace by measuring both operational excellence via customary performance metrics, and soulful excellence via metrics that include impact on people, society, and the world at large. This is an optimistic and hopeful vision for the future of business and one that would be easy to embrace.

At the end of the day, visionary leaders:

- have a strategic focus
- take the initiative despite risks
- move deliberately past obstacles
- build alignment toward the vision

Servant Leaders

The concept of servant leadership is an ancient philosophy, often associated with religious traditions. Today it stands in contrast to an authoritarian, autocratic style of leadership. Servant leaders are seen as empathetic and practice a more participative style of decision making.

The highest priority of a servant leader is to encourage, support, and enable team members to reach toward their full potential and capabilities. In his book *Mandela's Way*, Richard Stengel describes how Nelson Mandela led from both the front and from the back, depending on what the situation required. To Mandela, what mattered was the outcome over the long term rather than the issue of the moment.

Within the African concept of *ubuntu,* humans are all part of a complex web where the "me" is always subordinate to the "we." A Zulu proverb, "A person is a person through other people," describes the idea, which seems compatible with the notion of servant leadership.

> A person is a person through other people.
> *–Zulu proverb*

Servant leaders put others first. The best leaders operate with a sense of profound respect for other people and are motivated by gratitude and appreciation for their efforts. They are focused on the value that different people with different strengths and unique abilities contribute to the team and to the end result. They are able to engender trust and to inspire the best in people, building relationships up, down, and across to create an environment of collaboration and joint accountability. The goal of servant leadership is empowerment; with a holistic perspective, servant leaders tend to view the world from the bottom of an inverted pyramid.

Many famous servant leaders come to mind, including Mandela, Martin Luther King Jr., Mother Teresa, and Mahatma Gandhi. But there are ordinary people who rise to the level of servant leadership as well.

As the executive vice president at California Bank & Trust, **Betty Rengifo Uribe** has been instrumental in creating a comprehensive initiative connecting minority and women business owners to valuable resources and financing options. Her community outreach activities include leadership roles in Junior Achievement, the Hispanic Outreach Taskforce, the Cal Asian Chamber and *Latina Style*. And she earned her BA and MBA as a single mom, finalizing her doctorate soon after marriage, while balancing those studies with her impressive career advancement.

Values-based leadership was the subject of her dissertation, and for it she interviewed senior leaders in financial services, military leaders, and entrepreneurs. She wanted to understand not only *how* to lead in a way that is consistent with what is important to you, but how to spread that into your organization or team. She wondered what consciousness leaders had about their level of impact: What it is about you that inspires others? How does doing the right thing fit with your purpose in life? Is your level of motivation internal or external?

Betty believes that leadership starts with your way of *being* and that you have a choice of being a victim or taking ownership by being grateful for your gifts and making an impact with them. Her story reflects this choice.

Betty was born in Bogota, Colombia, and led a very privileged life until she was twelve. She was "daddy's little girl" and, according to her brothers, conceited. Her father was a wealthy businessman, and she and her brothers had everything they wanted—new toys and a brand-new wardrobe every year. That was because her mother gave away all their toys and clothes to the destitute street cleaners when she invited them into her home to feed them.

When Betty was twelve, her mother made a decision to leave Colombia to escape the domestic abuse that was common in that time and place and move to the United States. The children all opted to go with their mother.

Within twenty-four hours, she and her family went from very rich to very poor, depending on the kindness of strangers in a world they did not know, in a culture they did not understand, and in a language they could not speak. Their food came from the church and their clothes from garage sales. Betty, who had always been popular, began to feel inadequate as she became the brunt of jokes and ridicule about her accent and clothing. And even when they had nothing, her mother continued with her generosity to others, sharing their clothes, their food, and their beds with those even more unfortunate. These were Betty's early lessons about servant leadership.

The importance of education was another clear theme in Betty's upbringing. As she paid her own way through college with two jobs, she studied and worked hard to get ahead. When she became the youngest branch manager at Wells Fargo and received a large bonus for her results, her first call was to her mother, working in a factory at that time. She told her that today would be her last day in the factory, that she would never have to work again, and that the two of them were going on a first-class trip to Mexico.

Betty and her father had written to each other every week. From him, she learned about the strength to transform oneself. When she returned to Colombia for his funeral, she was overwhelmed by the sheer number of mourners; he had clearly helped so many people in his life and made a positive impact.

Embedded in Betty's DNA are lessons of transformational leadership from her dad and true servant leadership from her mom. She aspires to be a fraction of what her parents were. Her motto is about giving and loving unconditionally, and it is the way she works, the way she raises her own children, and the way she leads her life. She knows that the gift is in the giving and that money does not make one happy; making an impact and fulfilling a higher purpose are what bring happiness.

In order to teach her own children the values that drive her, she wanted to provide experiences that would impress and inspire them. She traveled to the poorest areas of India with her son and to Mexico with her daughters, suitcases filled with gifts for others. They learned the gift is in the giving.

Betty is deliberate and intentional about how to inspire others. She knows that talk is cheap and often filled with empty promises. She knows that actions communicate your message the loudest: "Your actions are so loud I can't hear what you're saying." She knows that she is not perfect, but she works on herself every day. She knows what's important, and she wants her actions and behaviors to be congruent with her espoused values.

Betty is an inspiration to all who know her or watch her or listen to her. She is a true servant leader, encouraging, supporting, and enabling others to reach their full potential and capabilities.

Servant leaders are confident but also humble. To be a servant leader, you must dedicate yourself to others, and this is not easy for most people. In *The Five Levels of Leadership,* John Maxwell writes about the fifth or Pinnacle Level, where a true legacy is created within an organization through the development of the next level of leaders. And this only happens when the leader is able to see people not just as they are, but as they could be. In this way, the servant leader makes a significant contribution.

At the end of the day, servant leaders:

- put others first, encouraging development of strengths
- focus on the long-term implications of their work
- continually build relationships, trust, and empowerment
- see themselves as supporters and enablers

Transformational Leaders

The attributes of a transformational leader include passion, persistence, and perseverance. Transformational leaders are driven by a cause or a purpose that is larger than they are. Within that belief is a certainty that they cannot do it alone, so they are inclusive and collaborative. And they learn to build bridges wherever they are needed. They put one foot in front of the other with the confidence that the next step will be revealed to them.

All leadership takes courage, but transformational leaders are the most courageous of all because they challenge the status quo, the traditional power structure, and sometimes even core values and beliefs. They do this from a sense of inner knowing that there is a better way and there is no time like the present to forge it.

The best transformational leaders exhibit a great balance between patience and impatience, knowing that sustainable change takes time. Sometimes it's like "struggling uphill with a heavily loaded cart against a strong wind," according to Guo Jianmei, recognized for her decades-long work for women's rights in China. Fueled by a fierce determination, transformational leaders are often defined by the way they handle setbacks and obstacles.

When Sunitha Krishnan was fifteen years old, she was gang-raped by eight men. As she struggled to make sense of what happened, she felt isolated and ashamed. She wondered if she had been at fault and coped with learning to overcome the stigma of disgrace in a country where many young women suffering the same fate commit suicide. Sunitha refused to see herself as a victim. Realizing that others could not pull her out of the darkness, she looked within and found the strength to turn her pain into determination and commitment. She vowed to help end the sexual exploitation of women and children in India.

Sunitha founded Prajwala (Eternal Flame), a nongovernmental organization in Hyderabad, India, that rescues children from pornography, sex tourism, and prostitution—and helps them to become survivors through programs centered on restoring their dignity and independence. It operates a residential shelter and schools that provide vocational training, life-skills development, and psychosocial support. Partnering with community members, local law enforcement, and national media, Prajwala also focuses on political and legal advocacy and emphasizes prevention through massive education campaigns.

Since its inception, and despite physical, psychological, and economic challenges, the organization has rescued over ninety-five hundred victims, housed more than five hundred survivors, sensitized millions to the issue of sex trafficking, and successfully lobbied for legal reform.

Sunitha is that rare breed of leader who committed her life as a full-time volunteer to Prajwala, even though she has been brutally attacked a dozen times and frequently receives death threats. She refuses to be intimidated by those who would silence her to protect the lucrative business of human trafficking; she is "determined to create a world where human dignity is protected and life is never bought, traded, or discarded."

Sunitha's is one of the powerfully inspirational stories told by Alyse Nelson, president and CEO of Vital Voices, in her book *Vital Voices*. These are unforgettable accounts of the brave visionary women who triumph over extraordinary struggles, risking everything to make the world a better place, lifting millions of people in the process.

The Vital Voices Global Partnership is a nonpartisan, nonprofit, nongovernmental organization that had its roots as a U.S. government initiative following the United Nations Fourth World Conference on Women in Beijing. Fueled by then-First Lady Hillary Rodham Clinton's bold proclamation that "women's rights are human rights," it was founded on the principle that when women progress, whole societies are able to move forward.

In its first fifteen years, Vital Voices has worked with over 14,000 women leaders from more than 140 countries. It has become "a global movement that transcends national, cultural, economic and political divides," as it amplifies the voices of women, supporting their efforts to make significant global change. It recognizes women as engines of economic growth and social progress.

Having interviewed a diversity of women from all corners of the globe and representing a range of backgrounds and experiences, Alyse Nelson expresses enormous respect, admiration, and gratitude for the different way these women lead. She offers the core practices that position women leaders as multipliers with the unique ability to effectively address many of humanity's most pressing problems.

These include a motivation to lead change that is more of a driving force, often born from overcoming enormous adversity, as Sunitha has. Often the motive is the result of strong roots in the community and a desire to listen and include those whose voices have been silenced.

Women have created sustainable change by breaking through and bridging the gaps that have typically divided people in order to build trust based on shared values—women like those in Northern Ireland who came together to put an end to the "sickening cycle of useless violence" by organizing peaceful projects and rallies, igniting a movement across the country.

They have brought bold ideas to life by thinking big and taking bold action, as in the example of a Brazilian graffiti artist who has used her art as a means to communicate the problem of domestic violence, previously considered a "private issue."

Recognizing that power expands when it is shared, the women represented in *Vital Voices* operate as agents of change with a pay-it-forward philosophy. The way they make a difference is by lifting others and recognizing that the world is a better place when everyone participates and every voice is heard.

As transformational leaders, they understood that there is no perfect time to begin leading. They led from where they stood, with limited resources and very little support. They each made a choice to step into leadership, fill the gap, and make things happen. They realized, as Bo Eason said, "…No one's coming. It's up to us—you and me."

At the end of the day, transformational leaders:

- are driven by a cause bigger than themselves
- understand that perseverance is the difference between failure and success
- are committed and passionate bridge builders
- lead from where they stand, even without support or resources

How Do You Lead?

Each of us has the exciting opportunity to choose the type of leader we want to be. Much of that choice may be based on innate and natural strengths, or even those abilities and qualities that are nourished and matured through life experiences and events. There is no "right" way to lead. And in fact not every leader clearly falls into one specific category. More and more, we see hybrid leaders who take qualities of each of the five categories of leadership.

> On the journey of life, there are always people ahead of you from whom you can learn, and people behind you who you can teach and help and support.

On the journey of life, there are always people ahead of you from whom you can learn, and people behind you who you can teach and help and support. Leading others is a gift. It is one you are born with, one that can be developed throughout life, and one that should readily and happily be offered to others. We all need guidance and support and people who are willing to push us and inspire us to reach levels of success that were once considered unreachable.

Each of us can be a trailblazer for someone else, like Gloria, Kathy, Karen, or Amna. It requires the courage to take risks, to overcome fears, and to move forward with confidence even when you don't know exactly where the road will lead.

And, as a leader, you are always a role model whether you realize it or not. People are watching you to see what to do and what to say. Your actions speak louder than your words—to your team, your friends, and your family. Jerry Rice may have been unaware of the impact he had on Bo Eason. But Bo understands that it is up to each of us to choose to be the leader we are capable of being. You get to decide how to show up.

You can identify and embrace your own level of motivation, the area of your focus, and your desire to connect, like Betty.

You can follow your dream and your vision, even when it represents a contrary point of view, like Joey Reiman has done, challenging the very status quo of business metrics.

You can recognize the opportunity to make a difference and choose to act or speak out when it's unpopular or even dangerous, as Sunitha and the other courageous leaders represented in *Vital Voices* have done.

You can decide to have a positive impact on the lives of others—in big or small ways. So take the time to survey your inner fabric and leadership DNA. And then start your own journey to elevate others. Because at the end of the day, leaders are much like elevators: if they push the right buttons, they will help take people to higher levels.

☞ Usable Insights

- There are many types of leaders and many different types of situations where leadership comes into play. Anyone can be a leader.
- Five different categories demonstrate the ways that ordinary people may rise to the occasion:
  - **Trailblazers** who pave the wave by challenging the status quo
  - **Role models** who lead deliberately by example
  - **Visionaries** who see the future clearly and drive toward it
  - **Servant leaders** who inspire, enable and support others
  - **Transformational leaders** who create sustainable, high impact change

Action Steps

1. Based on the key strengths you identified in Chapter 2, determine what type of leadership most closely resembles the way you lead.
2. Choose a type of leadership that you aspire to further develop. Reread the description, examples and list of key qualities to determine specific areas to focus your development.

Chapter 5

Thoughts Lead to Actions:
Five Steps to Make It Happen

You are what you do, not what you say you'll do.
—C.G. Jung

As you read the stories of each of the leaders in the prior chapter, with whom did you most closely relate? Whose story most resonated within your heart and soul? You may have noticed how each of their acts of leadership and the way they were expressed were entirely unique. Each leader has his or her own journey and path. Some were placed in a position of leadership while others were driven by an inner force to take a leadership role. And while each type of leader may be described by different traits and characteristics, there is often overlap from one type of leader to another.

There are as many styles of leadership as there are leaders. Each leader is a distinct mix of background experiences, abilities, behavioral styles, and attitudes that form his or her unique perspective on leadership. At some point each leader makes the choice to take action in order to further a cause or achieve an objective. And in your own leadership journey you will do this many times as well. However, even before choosing to act comes the initial thought or idea that ultimately leads to action. If you want to be more deliberate about your actions, being deliberate about your thoughts is a great place to start.

Having a process for thinking, reflecting, and ultimately acting on your thoughts and ideas will elevate the level of your own leadership thinking and help you derive more benefit from it. It will increase the intention and practice of being more deliberate with your thinking.

> Simplicity is the ultimate sophistication.
> —Michelangelo

With all the challenging complexity in the world today, when someone is able to cut through the density to create a simple formula, framework, or template to guide you through something you are learning or doing, it's a thing of beauty. As Michelangelo taught, "Simplicity is the ultimate sophistication."

So consider this deceptively Simple 5-Step Process for Turning Thoughts into Action™. Look at it as the bridge between talking the talk and walking the walk. Ultimately it will help you turn deliberate thoughts into actionable achievement.

Later, when you learn how to utilize questions as the secret weapon of leaders, this process will be a useful way to work through the questions, reflect on your thoughts, and determine whether or not you want to follow through and take action. With that said, here you go:

The Simple 5-Step Process™

1. Write it down
2. Share it
3. Test it
4. Get feedback
5. Implement it

The Simple 5-Step Process™
(for turning thoughts and ideas into action)

Step 1: Write it down

The act of writing actually helps clarify your thinking. It also allows you to go back at a later date and see if what you wrote still reflects your current thinking.

In addition, the act of writing releases clutter in your brain. I will often begin workshops by having participants write down whatever is on their minds—problems, challenges, opportunities, to-do lists, etc.—as a way to clear their heads and make room for the learning about to occur. It is remarkably effective in helping people to be more present. And you can do this anytime you want to do some creative, strategic thinking.

As a business coach, I often teach clients who feel overwhelmed to document steps of even the simplest daily and weekly activities. Initially resistant, they quickly learn that writing down these routines actually frees up their minds toward more creative, innovative, or challenging tasks. Once the steps are in writing, they don't have to "think" about each one each time. This ultimately contributes to greater productivity for the entire team.

Another great productivity trick is to spend five minutes at the end of the workday writing down the priorities for the next day. This not only allows you to hit the ground running the next morning but also frees your mind from the stress of endlessly mulling over issues and challenges—often at the expense of much-needed sleep.

Along with writing down the answer to the questions you will learn to ask yourself, you may want to set an intention or a specific action plan, writing down the steps required to achieve success. Additionally, it may be helpful to visualize your success in following through on the action. Close your eyes, see it in the present moment, and describe it in greater detail (in writing).

If your intention is to create a lasting change for yourself, writing your intention in the form of an affirmation also provides additional energy toward achieving it.

In her book on writing affirmations, *Change Almost Anything in 21 Days*, Ruth Fishel provides the characteristics that make an affirmation effective:

1. It must be **positive** (usually start with the words "I am" or "I am in the process of ")—avoiding words like not, don't, or won't.
2. It must be said and felt with **passion and power**, like you really believe it.
3. It must be said in the **present** moment (as if it were already true).
4. It must be **possible.**
5. It must be **personal** (in other words, it cannot be about someone else).

Here's an example of an affirmation I wrote to help me overcome my sense of being disorganized: "I AM organized, efficient, and productive in my work and in my life." I wrote it down and read it to myself several times a day.

And now, whenever someone refers to me as organized, I have to consciously stop myself and acknowledge that he or she is correct.

Repeating affirmations is a powerful way to propel your success in making a lasting change. Ruth's book is full of amazing case studies.

Why not try it now? Take something you want to change and write it in the form of an affirmation. Remember to be positive, passionate, in the present, possible, and personal. Then repeat it frequently and with conviction. You will be surprised at how well this works. It has been said that the two most powerful words in the English language are "I am." The reason why? Because the mind takes it as a command and begins to operate on whatever we say after that. After writing down your thoughts or responses or affirmations, the next step is to share it.

Step 2: Share it

Like writing, sharing your thoughts will help you gain greater clarity. There is great value in sharing an idea or thought with someone who can act as a sounding board. Using a trusted advisor or trained coach for this purpose will add even greater value.

That person may ask clarifying questions, play the devil's advocate, or help you formulate a greater level of detail around your thinking. If your thinking is too detailed, they may help you to step back and see the bigger picture and to create context.

They may also help in connecting your thoughts to other thoughts, to see patterns or other possibilities that exist.

The simple act of saying it out loud gives you the chance to hear how it sounds outside your own head.

How often have you had the experience of saying something out loud that sounds ridiculous or surprising or even brilliant? Articulating your thought—giving it voice—makes it more real. It creates a new level of reality.

I recently worked with a team of women to create an event for our local chamber of commerce to kick off the New Year with the theme "Magnifying Success." As the facilitator for the event, I asked members of the team to test some of the activities we would be using during the session. Each was asked to share a success story from the prior year that created an impact on her thinking or perspective. The stories were powerful and inspiring.

Jennifer was struggling to come up with a story; she felt she had "missed" most of the prior year because she had been fighting breast cancer. But her light bulb went off when I pointed out that this was quite a success story and asked what she had learned from the experience. As Jennifer started to recount the life lessons from her journey of recovery, she realized that, by acknowledging, owning, and sharing her success, it was a powerful story of inspiration to others.

Jennifer spoke passionately about "building a bridge" from one step to the next in the process and then realized she could apply this same approach to some challenges she and her business partner were having in their business. Using the wisdom gained from her very personal journey, she was able to leverage her success to create success in another area of her life. Sharing can be a powerful way to move your thinking forward.

By the way, sharing your thoughts is a great way to demonstrate your *willingness*—to yourself and others—to challenge your own thinking.

Which brings us to the next step.

Step 3: Test it

When a new thought is introduced for the first time, I like to recommend something I call "trying it on."

This can be something new that occurred to you for the first time, something that was introduced to you by someone else, or the act of introducing a new thought to someone else.

In any event, I suggest giving room to the possibility that this may be a random thought that doesn't have much value or sustainability— or it could be a thought worth pursuing, worth thinking through, or worth debating.

"Trying it on" is the process of acting "as if" the thought were valid or true or maybe even brilliant. And then just seeing what comes up.

Sharing the thought with someone is one way to test it. But the simple act of observing the world with that thought in mind can be equally revealing.

Here's an example of what I mean: can you think of a time when someone made an observation about a person you both know that was totally outside of your experience with that person? It could be something simple, like the number of times they use a particular phrase such as "you know." Or it could be something like a character trait that you have never noticed.

Someone brings it to your attention, and initially you may be surprised; but once you focus your attention on it, you can't believe you missed it!

Let's look at a more complex example.

Imagine you've started a new job, one that you are very excited about. Even though the environment is very different from the one you had in your old job, you feel certain that your energy and enthusiasm to make a difference will help you to be successful quickly.

What you learn, to your dismay, is that the new team is not at all receptive to your ideas and contributions.

This was the case with Anita when she called me in tears. She was so frustrated and hurt and angry that she couldn't really think straight.

After having her take a few deep breaths to calm down, I asked her to try thinking differently about the situation.

Instead of forging ahead with her enthusiasm for her ideas, I asked her to slow down and try a different approach: first, find the person most affected by that idea and ask that person for some advice. Share your observation, challenge, or frustration—and how you feel about the situation—then ask how she would handle it. What advice might she have?

This was clearly a new way for Anita to think about her situation. Instead of acting as the expert with all the answers and ideas, she positioned herself as the new kid trying to find her way and looking for help and support from others who had been there longer and had more experience in that environment.

It was not easy for Anita to do this. It required her to think differently. It required her to check her ego at the door. But it worked beautifully.

This was an example of "trying it on." I did not ask her to commit to using this approach forever, just temporarily to see if she could win over some of her coworkers. This initial step back and new approach provided some much needed leverage.

The point here is that you can have a new thought and act on it—in subtle or noncommittal ways—to see how it works and whether it has value for making a permanent change in the way you do things.

The purpose of testing out your thought, of course, is to get feedback.

Step 4: Get feedback

The whole point of sharing your thought and testing it is to obtain valuable feedback that can help you to further refine it.

Feedback falls into two categories: positive and negative. We all like positive feedback—praise from others, getting the results we wanted, inner feelings of happiness or pleasure, satisfied customers, and so forth.

Negative feedback in the form of criticism, complaints, and feelings of inner conflict or pain is harder to accept. And yet it is *so valuable*. Amazing transformations occur when we are willing as leaders to challenge our own thinking and to accept negative feedback as a way to improve our thinking.

> Amazing transformations occur when we are willing as leaders to challenge our own thinking and to accept negative feedback as a way to improve our thinking.

When was the last time you tried to offer feedback and the person was totally defensive about it? Maybe they argued about your point of view, or made an excuse or even blamed someone else.

My favorite experience with this happened at our local diner. On a frigid winter night, we called to order two hot turkey dinners to go. When I got home, I discovered two hot roast beef dinners instead. I called the diner and was told, "No, you ordered roast beef."

"I don't eat roast beef," I said. "I wanted turkey."

And the guy said, "Well, you ordered roast beef."

"I need to bring it back and get turkey because I don't eat roast beef."

His response: "Fine. Bring it back."

By this time I was pretty angry as I put my winter coat and boots back on and drove back to the diner. They took the bag and disappeared into the back without a word.

When they returned with the turkey, I said. "Well?"

"Well, what?"

"Well, how about an apology? How about giving me my money back for making me drive all the way home and all the way back again on this freezing cold winter night?"

"Okay. Sorry. We can give you the turkey or give you your money, not both."

So I asked, "Who can give me my money back?"

"Only the manager."

"Let me talk to him."

"He's not here."

"Get him on the phone."

Now, mind you, I was making quite a scene in the diner. My voice was getting louder as my frustration grew and my patience disappeared. People had stopped talking and were observing this interaction.

The manager would not speak to me on the phone. He did tell the person to give my money back.

No one offered a genuine apology or any further compensation for the inconvenience.

They were convinced it was my mistake, not theirs. They thought I was a pain in the butt. But, seriously, what are the chances that I ordered roast beef when I don't even eat roast beef?

They were not open to the feedback. They were defensive, protecting their turf.

There were all sorts of better ways to handle the situation if they had been open to the feedback and interested in retaining a loyal customer.

Needless to say, I have told that story dozens of times to individuals and large groups. Though I'm sure they didn't even notice, I have not been back to the diner since.

How do you handle negative feedback?

Some people take it personally. Some people just cave in and quit. Some people get angry. Some ignore the feedback altogether.

Feedback is simply the valuable exchange of *information*. And it is such a powerful tool for continuous improvement. Even though it can hurt, it provides such an opportunity to help you get from point A to point B faster or more effectively.

Think about an area in your life right now where you can use some feedback. Write it down. I could use some feedback on _____. Put a star next to it. Then start asking people for feedback and record that too. Reflect on it and, if appropriate, act on it.

One of the simplest ways to do this is to ask, "On a scale of one to ten, how am I doing with X?" If the answer is anything less than ten, ask a follow-up question: "What would make it a ten?" This is simple and powerful and gives you a way to measure your progress.

Learn to welcome feedback and learn to use it. Learn to ask for it. Make it a habit and part of your daily routine. Be sure to make it safe for people to give you feedback. Feedback is a gift, especially for leaders.

You are better off knowing what people are thinking because then you can do something about it. You can improve your performance, your effectiveness, your relationships—and your results. And that way people can get their turkey when they order it.

It's important to recognize that feedback is just someone's perception at a point in time—no more, no less. Not all feedback is accurate or helpful, and you need to consider the source. You need to look for patterns.

One of my favorite tools for leadership feedback is the multi-rater assessment known as a "360," which measures perceptions from different angles about a leader's skills and behaviors. You are able to compare your own self-assessment against those of your boss, your peers, your direct reports, and others such as customers or suppliers.

My client Mike was shocked the first time he completed a 360 assessment. The feedback about the way he was coming across to others matched neither his own belief nor his intent, and it was pretty disturbing. Once he got past his initial reaction and turned his attention to making measurable improvement, he was able to appreciate how each of his constituents could interpret his behavior differently.

With clarity on how specific behaviors were perceived by others, Mike was able to identify key strengths on which to build. These included taking charge, showing confidence, and being approachable. He was also able to identify three other behaviors on which to focus attention and improvement that would create the biggest impact with others. These included communicating with clarity, showing diplomacy, and remaining open to input.

Mike's openness to the feedback and his willingness to change his behavior have made him a much more effective leader. In fact, he is seen as one of the high potential individuals being groomed for more responsibility and future opportunities. He routinely completes 360 assessments to identify his next area of focus for improvement.

An aspect of feedback that is often overlooked is your own gut feelings or instincts. This is your *internal feedback*. When you are listening externally to what others are telling you, be sure to listen internally as well. What is your body telling you? What do you feel? What is your gut instinct?

Can you remember a time when you didn't feel quite right about something? How did that show up for you? A lump in your throat? Tightness in your chest? Or a feeling in the pit of your stomach? Learn to recognize whatever that "feeling" is for you. Pay attention and respect it.

Feedback is an important element to consider before you go to the next step in the process.

Step 5: Implement it

Once you've shared it, tested it, and gotten feedback about it, you are then ready to take action. You are ready to implement.

Having thought about your actions in advance, you are now in a better position to get the outcome you actually intend and the result you want. If you've been writing and sharing and testing, you have the beginnings of an action plan. You may need to further refine it before you jump in, but the fact that you have feedback about your idea or thought will make you more confident as you implement.

Thinking leads to clarity. Clarity allows you to focus your attention, your energy, and your time. Your implementation will be more efficient and your level of personal productivity will be greater. As a leader, when you model this type of simple yet powerful process, you help others become more effective and more productive as well.

This Simple 5-Step Process for Turning Thoughts into Action will help you as you learn how to lead from the inside out and improve your level of leadership thinking. It provides a simple yet powerful tool for reflecting on your thoughts and ideas and working through them to refine, improve, and gather support for them. You will benefit by being more confident in the actions you choose to take as a result of the process.

> Only when we transcend the inside and deliver it to the outside can something as small as a few seeds grow into something as large as a forest.

We all want to turn our thoughts into action. We all dream of manifesting our internal hopes and desires into something tangible and external. Every exciting accomplishment started with a thought, or a seed. As that seed was planted and nourished, it turned into something so large that it simply couldn't be contained. It had to sprout and grow on the outside of each of us. We all have the seeds of leadership planted within. But only when thoughts become actions can lives be changed, mountains be climbed, and pinnacles be reached. Only when we transcend the inside and deliver it to the outside can something as small as a few seeds grow into something as large as a forest.

☞ Usable Insights

- The Simple 5-Step Process™ is a powerful methodology for turning thoughts and ideas into action. Use it to develop greater clarity in your thinking.
- Be open to both external and internal feedback. This will have a transformational impact on your leadership effectiveness.
- The process can be used to solve problems and evaluate opportunities, leading to better decisions. Better decisions will increase your credibility and influence.

👣 Action Steps

1. Choose a current problem or opportunity that requires a decision and follow all 5 Steps of the process to solve and decide. Be sure to journal your thoughts during each step.
2. Define an area in your life where you can use more feedback. Sit quietly and ask yourself for help. Write down your thoughts; share them and test them with others for additional perspective.
3. Identify something you want to change. Using the guidelines in the chapter, create an affirmation for yourself as if you have already made the change. Make a note on your calendar to repeat it three times a day for the next 21 days.

Chapter 6

Framing It Up:
Mindset Musts of
an Influential Leader

A man is the product of his thoughts; what he thinks, he becomes.
—Mahatma Gandhi

C arol Dweck is a world-renowned psychologist, research scientist, and professor at Stanford University. In her groundbreaking book *Mindset, the New Psychology of Success*, she describes how to fulfill our potential in school, at work, as parents, and in both personal and professional relationships. Her research shows that "the view you adopt for yourself profoundly affects the way you lead your life. It can determine whether you become the person you want to be and whether you accomplish the things you value."

The view you adopt for yourself profoundly affects the way you lead your life. It can determine whether you become the person you want to be and whether you accomplish the things you value.

—*Carol Dweck*

Your mind is constantly monitoring and interpreting everything that happens to you. The resulting mindset frames your conscious or subconscious internal dialogue, further guiding your interpretation of any situation. The World English Dictionary describes a *mindset* as "the ideas and attitudes with which a person approaches a situation." Are you aware of the ideas and attitudes with which you approach leadership? If not, together we will begin to focus your attention on identifying and sculpting your attitude.

Cultivating a mindset is a lot like planting a garden. You create an environment that is nurturing and ready to support growth when you prepare the soil, removing weeds and stones and adding fertilizer before you plant. Once you add seeds, and introduce water and sunlight, plants begin to develop, breaking through the soil to flourish in a nutrient-rich environment.

Likewise, when you are deliberate about choosing your mindset, you prepare your mind to be receptive to thoughts and ideas that will nourish and support your own growth. You create an environment that nurtures your development. You plant the seeds, you feed and fertilize, and you promote progress, expansion, and change.

The mindset of an influential leader includes these four essential mindsets:

1. *Take 100 percent responsibility for your life, your leadership, and your thinking.*

2. ***Lead with an open mind and an open heart.***
3. ***Be proactive, deliberate, and intentional about your thinking.***
4. ***Commit to lifelong learning and development about leadership.***

Together these elements form an environment within which you can propel your own growth as well as the growth of those you influence, just as the carefully cultivated garden supports its crops to harvest.

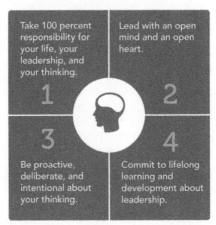

The mindset musts of an influential leader

Take 100 percent responsibility for your life, your leadership, and your thinking. **1**	Lead with an open mind and an open heart. **2**
Be proactive, deliberate, and intentional about your thinking. **3**	Commit to lifelong learning and development about leadership. **4**

Mindset Must #1: Take 100 percent responsibility for your life, your leadership, and your thinking

I was training to be a business coach the first time I was introduced to the concept of taking full responsibility for myself, for my circumstances, and for my results. The sudden awareness of two distinct patterns of behaving "above or below the line" created an "aha!" moment for me. It was an eye-opener that completely changed my pattern of thought as I recognized that some people always blame others or point to the circumstances to justify the situation, have an excuse for everything that goes wrong, and at worst act in total denial of their own part in their situation.

Thinking about people I had known or worked with who fell into the category of living "below the line," I realized how much this prevented them from achieving their best work, their most meaningful relationships, and overall success in life. But I was simultaneously encouraged by the idea that others took full ownership, full accountability, and full responsibility for themselves, for their results, and for their circumstances. I realized that these people were not only the ones I most enjoyed hanging out with, but also those who contributed to their own success.

Right then and there I made my own decision to live "above the line" from that point onward. Sharing this concept with friends and family made for some interesting observations and dialogue. It also served to increase my own awareness of behavior in myself and others.

As I began to include this learning in all my workshops and seminars, as well as share it with individual clients, I could see more light bulbs go off. As I presented this concept to others, I gained additional perspective on the impact living above or below the line had on people in the workplace, in the family, and among friends. The learning grew deeper into my spirit. It changed my behavior, it changed my attitude, and it changed my thinking. This one simple concept was completely transformational for me.

What about you? When you think about the people in your life, how often do they have a reason or excuse for their current situation? How often do they blame others or something outside of themselves rather than looking inwardly? And how many people do you know who are dwelling in complete denial?

Here's the big question: What about your own behavior? How often do you fall below the line? And when that happens, how quickly can you pull yourself back up above it? As a leader, can you see how your own behavior and attitude and thinking can impact the behavior and attitude and thinking of the people around you?

Learning to fully understand the impact of and fully appreciate the value of mindset is extremely powerful. No matter what you do for a living, your mindset will ultimately determine your level of success. And as a leader your mindset will contribute to the success of others as well. Learning to think like an influential leader means taking 100 percent responsibility for your thinking.

Why is clarity of thinking so important for leaders? Because the rest of the world is looking to you to show the way. This is why Mindset Must #1 for influential leaders is taking 100 percent responsibility for your life, your leadership, and your thinking. You may feel you already do this; I did too—until I opened my heart and mind and realized I could do more and be more. I challenge you to take 100 percent responsibility for your life, including your:

- Learning
- Actions
- Attitude
- Results
- Leadership – for the way you connect with others and the way you influence them.

This means you don't make excuses, you don't blame others, and you don't deny your part when something is not going the way you want. Instead, you take ownership and hold yourself accountable. And you model the way for others to do the same. In order to move in the direction of 100 percent responsibility, it is necessary to open both your mind and your heart.

Mindset Must #2: Lead with an
open mind and an open heart

Open your mind. No really, open it wide. This means being completely receptive to the learning process, recognizing that it's constant and never-ending. Learning is blocked when you close your mind. You miss possibilities and overlook opportunities.

Remember, if you are paying attention, each and every experience you have can contribute to who you become as a leader. And when you improve yourself, everything around you also improves. As a leader your mindset becomes a model for others to follow, and when openness is present there is more learning, more creativity, and more progress. But ultimately there are better results.

Open your heart. An open heart invites growth and amazing leadership potential. But it starts with shedding the layer of judgment and harshness with others. This can be difficult, but it is important. It allows for the full benefit of the experiences you have. You will find positive results when you approach the actions and behaviors of others with the idea that they are doing the best they can in that particular moment.

Often we automatically assign negative motives to the behaviors of others and then respond defensively with anger and frustration. "Assuming positive intent" is a great way to counteract our human tendency to believe what we want to believe. When you are able to change that default filter to a more positive one, you open your heart to other possibilities.

In their book *Decisive*, Chip Heath and Dan Heath provide examples of how this type of thinking can lead us to better decisions by testing our assumptions. Indra Nooyi, the chairman and CEO of PepsiCo, cited "assuming positive intent" to *Fortune* as the best advice she ever received, because it helped her to see things she did not see.

Consider the story of Sherman Smith, an assistant coach of the 2013 Super Bowl champion Seattle Seahawks. Smith has been a coach with three NFL football teams. Before that, he played for eight years in the league after winning three mid-American Conference titles as Miami University's (Ohio) first black quarterback.

As Smith grew up in Youngstown, Ohio, his father asked him what he wanted to do after high school graduation. His plans were modest: get a job in the steel mill, live in the nearby apartment complex (the projects), and drive a nice car.

His father opened his mind and opened his heart when he took him for a tour of the area with this admonition: "Don't buy into the lie that this is the only place you can live and this is the only job you can have. Don't buy into the lie that you cannot live in the upscale neighborhood and be a teacher, doctor, lawyer, or president of the United States."

As he went on to college, his mother also counseled him to ignore the negative stereotypes that he would inevitably encounter, urging him to rise above them and make his own way and his own impact. She encouraged him to make the way easier for others.

Sherman Smith went on to create his own legacy as a player, as a coach, and as a parent to his own son, who also played football at Miami U. His coaching goes beyond X's and O's to include the teaching of enduring values and challenging his players to become the type of person they want to be. He knows that the game will end but the values taught can live forever. He lives and leads with an open mind and an open heart. This is an essential part of the influential leader's mindset, especially if you are deliberate about your role as a leader like Sherman Smith.

Mindset Must #3: Be proactive, deliberate, and intentional about your thinking

How you approach a situation can make all the difference in the outcome you get. Imagine working for the same company for twenty-two years.

You've worked your way up to a leadership role and feel good about the contribution you make to the company's success and to the team members you lead. Then you learn that your company has been acquired and chances are good that your business unit—and your job—will be eliminated in the process. What do you do?

That was the situation Cindy was facing when she attended one of my leadership workshops. She was bitter and angry. She couldn't believe how easily her company turned its back on loyal employees like her. There would be no severance or other support. And she was scared. She knew how tough the job market was. She didn't see how she could compete with all the younger, less expensive people looking for work in her industry. How would she buy groceries and pay the rent?

I asked Cindy to take a step back and try to look at her circumstances differently. I encouraged her to think strategically: How could the situation be turned into an opportunity? What if she could look back on this experience a year from now and realize that it was beneficial to her?

We've all had painful experiences that, in retrospect, were blessings in disguise. Can you think of a time in your life that you gained something from a loss, learned something from a mistake or failure, or came through a tough challenge that boosted your confidence and self-esteem? It can be difficult to see through to the other side when you're in the middle of the loss, the mistake, or the challenge. But the good news is that, with practice, this can become your default behavior.

Most people faced with this situation would be bitter and angry, just like Cindy. But I want to share an important lesson I learned from a colleague of mine named Jack.

When I arrived in a new position, things were changing. The company was reorganizing and cutting expenses. People were being laid off and morale was horrible.

Everyone was angry: the people leaving were angry about losing their jobs, and the people staying were equally angry about having to absorb more of the workload.

Then there was Jack. Even though Jack was scheduled for a layoff, he came in every day with a smile on his face and just got to work. He wasn't distracted by the water cooler conversations and long coffee breaks his coworkers were taking. He was asking others how he could help them. He seemed to be in another reality altogether.

So I asked him: "Jack, what's going on? How do you do it? Why do you do it?"

"Simple," he told me. "When I'm gone, I want to be missed. I want them to realize they made a mistake. I want them to remember me as a hardworking, positive guy. And even if I never get called back, I want to leave on good terms, and I want to feel like I did the right thing right up until the end. I want to feel good about myself, knowing I did my very best."

Jack was a great role model for others. Some thought he was crazy but others adopted his philosophy, and that made for a better experience for everyone. Jack made a difference and an impact. And, by the way, when the company started hiring again, Jack was the first person we called.

So, with Jack in mind, I challenged Cindy to think through how she wanted to leave her company. Here are some of the questions I asked her to think about:

1. What image do you want to project as you go through this process?
2. How do you want to be perceived?
3. What do you want people to remember about you? Your bosses? Your coworkers? Your team? Your customers? Your vendors? And what about the "new guys"?

4. Think about what you could possibly gain out of the experience itself. What might you learn in the process?

5. As a leader, what behavior and attitude could you model for others?

6. Finally, how do you want to feel about yourself throughout the process and at the end of it?

When I followed up with Cindy a month later, she was a different person in a different place. She was positive and upbeat. She had a million ideas for what she would do next and was excited about the opportunity to pursue some of her dreams that had otherwise been put on hold.

Cindy also took her responsibility as team role model very seriously. She knew that her team would benefit by maintaining a positive attitude too, even as the world shifted beneath their feet. She worked hard at helping them find opportunities to pursue, and she advocated on their behalf. She felt good about that as well.

The new company had offered her a position, and though it involved a relocation that wasn't practical at the time, Cindy felt truly valued for her contribution and more optimistic about her prospects. Cindy's story is a great example of the value and benefit of taking time to analyze the situation and being *deliberate* and *intentional* about your approach.

How often have you noticed that many people in positions of leadership simply react? They react to problems or challenges. They react to circumstances or situations.

How many times have you reacted to something without first thinking? How often have you decided something without even being aware of the process you used to make a decision? And when was the last time you asked yourself the question: "What was I thinking?"

In *Blink*, Malcolm Gladwell explores the power of thinking without thinking. He looks at the process that differentiates great decisions made in the moment from some truly bad decisions, and he introduces the notion of "thin-slicing."

"Thin-slicing" is the art of filtering the very few factors that matter from the overwhelming number of variables in the mix. It's a fascinating concept, based on cutting-edge neuroscience and psychology. But, most important to us, it causes you to think differently about thinking.

> You are in a better position to make a decision "in the moment" when you spend time thinking.

You are in a better position to make a decision "in the moment" when you spend time thinking. Thinking allows you to be prepared for opportunities when they arise. It allows you to focus your attention, energy, and time on the game changers—the things that will make a difference.

You are able to achieve more when you spend time thinking about how you will direct your time, energy, and attention. You are able to live on purpose and then reap the benefits.

One benefit is the ability to determine what you want the outcome to be. The more specific you can be about this, the better. You will see how this works in chapter 8, when we discover the secret weapon of effective leaders.

Deliberate and proactive thinking allows you to figure out *how* to move in the direction of that outcome: What's the game plan? Who needs to do what by when?

Another benefit is to decide in advance how "success" will be measured. That way you will know it when you see it. You will have greater confidence you are leading yourself where you want to go and helping others by showing the way.

Along the way, deliberate and proactive thinking provides the chance to assess your own strengths and weaknesses, as well as the opportunities in a particular situation and any external threats that may prevent your success. When thinking precedes your actions, it helps by making your actions more deliberate and intentional rather than accidental or reactive. And that is why it's part of the essential mindset for an influential leader.

Mindset Must #4: Commit to lifelong learning and development about leadership

When I described my framework for leadership development—Learning to Lead from Within—in chapter 3, commitment was the central theme present in every part of the process of becoming a more effective leader. The level of commitment required to make the transition becomes clear when you compare the influential leader of today to the positional leader of the past. This is not a simple transaction. It is a lifelong process.

And when author, speaker, and online trainer Brendon Burchard told me "Your vision for yourself—and what's possible—should not be limited by your current knowledge and capabilities," he was challenging me. And now I'm challenging you to make your personal and professional development an evergreen practice and discipline. This is a significant commitment, one that will often take you beyond your comfort zone and require courage and persistence. It will also be rewarding beyond measure. There is always more to grow, further to go, and a bigger impact to make.

While studying the subject of full responsibility and accountability, I discovered *The Oz Principle*, written by Craig Hickman, Roger Connors, and Tom Smith. They describe accountability as "proactively seeing the reality of the situation, personally owning the circumstances, relentlessly looking for solutions and consistently following through," and they teach specific steps to achieve it. Then, in *Journey to the Emerald City*, the authors take it a step further, showing how implementing the

Oz Principle to create a "culture of accountability" can actually achieve a competitive advantage in an organization.

Imagine the impact you can have as a leader in shaping the culture of your organization, helping your team members take more responsibility and accountability both personally and jointly. Hickman, Connors, and Smith demonstrate how an organization's culture determines the results it achieves and how the results in turn reinforce the culture. And they describe the creation of culture as a leadership process. It is *not an event* and it is *not a program*. It's a *process that never ends*. And so it is with personal development and leadership development. It's a lifelong process too.

> Leadership development is a lot like establishing your own internal culture. It is not an event and it is not a program. It is a process that never ends.

Leadership development is a lot like establishing your own internal culture. Remember your internal culture is your personal psychology: how you think, how you feel, how you behave, and how you do the tough inside work of leadership. And, just as in an organization, you either manage your culture or it will manage you. When you invest in improving yourself, it impacts your whole life. And what could be a more important part of your thinking process than how you should lead yourself and how you should lead others?

In order to do that in the best possible way, you need to *take time to think*. Doing so will help you gain clarity of thought on how to help others think. And when you are able to do that, you have arrived. It's significant. It inspires and motivates you to do more—to be more. Although this is an ongoing personal journey for me, I'm sharing it because it's so important, especially now and especially here. We are all works in progress.

But remember the best leaders have the biggest impact.

Brendon Burchard teaches what separates the most successful personal development programs and the people we choose to follow as mentors. Here are the four things that the best leaders bring into your life:

First, the best leaders bring more **awareness** and more presence. They understand where you are and where you want to go and how to help you get there.

Second, they help you get to another level of **acceptance**. While understanding where you are, they also encourage you to accept it, to forgive yourself for your mistakes and failures—to learn—and to move on, to get over yourself as you were, and get on with who you can become. They help you to *know* you and to *be* you.

Third, the best leaders provide an appropriate level of **accountability.** They expect you to be accountable for your actions, for your results, and for your thinking. They want you to own where you are and acknowledge whether or not it is serving you in that moment.

Fourth, the best leaders inspire you to take **action**. They provide the motivational environment for you to do what you need to do to be successful, to get results, to make a difference.

Awareness. Acceptance. Accountability. Action.

When you think about the great leaders you have observed or experienced in your life, what was it that caused you to connect with them and to follow them? Just how did they influence you?

- How did they raise your **awareness**? Maybe they recognized a particular strength you have or an area needing improvement. Maybe they identified an opportunity you didn't see.

- How did they help you **accept** who and where you are and to move on from there?
- How did they encourage you to take **accountability**? Did they identify an area where you could take more responsibility for your life, for your performance, or for how you were being perceived by others?
- What **actions** did they inspire you to take? Maybe there were actions you were afraid to take and they helped you to set aside the doubt and summon the courage to move forward.

As a leader, you have the opportunity to bring these notions into your own life, as well as the lives of others. Your leadership legacy pushes you to think differently about your role as a leader, to challenge yourself and others, and to be an effective, impactful role model.

And it all builds from the mindset musts:

- Take 100 percent responsibility for your life, your leadership, and your thinking
- Lead with an open mind and an open heart.
- Be proactive, deliberate, and intentional about your thinking.
- Commit to lifelong learning and development about leadership.

Ask yourself how you can improve in each of these areas, recognizing that we are all works in progress, and ultimately make the commitment to improve. Your mindset has a big impact on both you and your success. But, more importantly, it has an impact on all the people you will influence in your life.

Like cultivating a garden that will flourish and prosper, creating a healthy mindset to support your growth as a leader will help develop the "landscape" around you. It will sprout other leaders and lead to a bountiful harvest for all. And it will encourage the healthy habits that make effective, influential leadership a reality for you and for those you lead.

☞ Usable Insights

- As a leader, your mindset is more important than your skill set. Deliberately choosing your mindset prepares you to be receptive to thoughts and ideas that will nourish and support your growth.
- Your internal culture is the result of developing thought patterns. Influential leaders:
  ○ Take 100 percent responsibility for life, leadership, and thinking.
  ○ Lead with an open mind and an open heart.
  ○ Are proactive, deliberate, and intentional about thinking.
  ○ Commit to lifelong learning and development about leadership.
- When you make time to think, you bring more awareness and presence to your leadership. This leads to more deliberate action and a bigger impact overall.

👣 Action Steps

1. On a scale of 1 to 10, rate the level responsibility you are taking in these areas: your learning, your actions, your attitudes, your results, and your leadership. Identify the steps you will take to move just one area closer to 10.
2. Consider one important relationship in your work. How can you develop that relationship by bringing more of an open heart and an open mind to it?

Chapter 7

Those That Came Before:
Six Critical Habits
of Successful Leaders

You may believe that you are responsible for what you do, but not for what you think. The truth is that you are responsible for what you think, because it is only at this level that you can exercise choice. What you do comes from what you think.

—Marianne Williamson

S ince your actions start with a thought or idea, thinking is where you can first exercise choice. And as you learned from the Simple 5-Step Process to Turn Thoughts into Action, you can turn your thoughts into deliberate, intentional actions that will deliver the results you want. By practicing the process again and again, it can eventually become a *habit* of thinking.

We usually associate habits with patterns of behavior that, through regular repetition, become automatic or unconscious. In the beginning the choices are made deliberately, and then at some point we stop thinking but continue doing. Researchers have learned why and how habits emerge and the science behind their mechanics. As a result we know that habits are powerful, often occurring without our permission and influencing our lives far more than we could ever realize.

Creating *habits of thought* means making deliberate, proactive choices about your thinking. This in turn supports your efforts to take full responsibility for your thinking and for managing your thinking so your thoughts don't control you. Honing this skill will ultimately improve your ability to connect with people and influence them as an effective leader.

How *do* leaders think? What's the difference between how they think and how other people think? And how can you use this information to develop your level of leadership thinking and overall effectiveness as a leader? These are some of the questions we will explore in this chapter.

From my experiences and observations over forty-plus years in business, I have identified six thinking patterns that distinguish influential leaders:

1. Leaders think with a success mindset.
2. Leaders think strategically as well as tactically.
3. Leaders use a framework to support their essential thinking.
4. Leaders think in terms of outcomes.
5. Leaders use a coach, mentor, or critical thinking partner to challenge their thinking.
6. Leaders actually schedule time to think.

Six patterns of thought that distinguish influential leaders

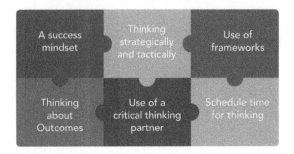

Leaders think with a success mindset

The best leaders actually view failure differently from others. They consider failure an inevitable part of the process of building success. They see it as a stepping stone and realize that failure is a necessary ingredient to growing and improving. They also understand that failure is an event and not a person.

In the last chapter we described the essence of the success mindset as Mindset Must #1: Take 100 percent responsibility for your life, your leadership, and your thinking. Living "above the line," taking ownership, and being accountable is essential to excelling as a role model. To do this, you have to avoid excuses, blaming, complaining, and looking outside yourself for the things you don't like in your life.

You also need to recognize the control you have over your thoughts, over the images you hold in your head, and over the actions you take as a result. This is all part of your opportune ability as a human being to *choose*. It is one of the most exciting aspects of leadership because you are in a better position to influence others based on *who you are* and not what you say or do.

Leaders think strategically as well as tactically

Strategic thinking is big-picture, visionary thinking. It's about understanding how all the moving parts fit together and considering the implications for you, for your team, and for your organization. Great leaders can think big while fully appreciating the importance of small details.

The thought process surrounding strategy begins with a clear foundation. In other words, it needs to be grounded. If you were building a house, you would start with a strong foundation. If you didn't, your house would not be stable. Similarly, if you don't start with your vision and core values to provide a strong and lasting beginning, how can you possibly expect to weather the inevitable storms? Operating without solid footing puts you and your team in a vulnerable position.

According to *Harvard Business Review*, "companies that enjoy enduring success have core values and a core purpose that remain fixed while their business strategies and practices endlessly adapt to a changing world."

This type of core ideology defines the enduring character of an organization over time, regardless of economic fluctuations, life cycles and product cycles, breakthroughs in technology and other threats, challenges and opportunities—and even changes in leadership.

Companies like Disney have a core purpose to "make people happy" and core values including "wholesomeness," "imagination," and "creativity." So much so that one can readily see and experience how these values play out in the way the company operates and the programs and products it creates. These values are truly foundational to who Disney is.

So ask yourself: What is your envisioned future, your vision? What is your core purpose? And what are the core values that guide your behavior, your decisions, and the actions you take? What are those guiding principles that you hold near and dear no matter where you are, where you go, and who you lead?

Knowing the answers to these questions allows you to say *no* in deference to a bigger *yes*. It guides your critical decision-making and helps you set priorities for both the long term and in the moment.

This starts with creating a strategic framework for your goals. Using a strategic process for yourself or with your team is enlightening and very empowering because it creates *alignment* around thinking. And alignment enables clarity. Alignment allows you to speed up the process of getting things done.

You lay the foundation for effective strategic planning and thinking when you start with core values and purpose. It is easier to identify strategic targets, develop your goals, and schedule the actions required to achieve them. This is an example of thinking—and planning—on both a strategic or visionary level and on a tactical level, where execution happens. Both are extremely important.

In chapter 8 you will have an opportunity to build your own foundation by identifying your core values and guiding principles.

Leaders think in terms of outcomes

When searching for clarity of purpose and direction, start by asking yourself the question: what is the outcome for which I am looking? This question brings clarity of purpose and direction. When you ask it of others, it helps to create engagement, agreement, and a path to effective collaboration.

In *The 7 Habits of Highly Effective People*, Stephen Covey calls this "beginning with the end in mind," one of the principles of personal leadership.

The whole process of planning and preparation for success comes into sharper focus whenever a client focuses on the desired outcome to think through a problem or situation he or she is facing. Asking "what is the outcome I'm looking for?" facilitates clarity. And when you have clarity of thought and clarity of intention, creating the roadmap to get the result you want is so much easier.

Frank runs an industrial construction business, working closely with property managers. One day he was very angry with one of his biggest and most profitable clients. It seems the client made a change in their internal process for reviewing bids that would require a lot more work on the part of Frank's estimators and project managers.

Frank was getting ready to meet with the client and really let him have it. They had been doing business together for many years, and Frank viewed the new requirements as a personal insult to the trust they had built over time.

I first asked Frank to consider what the reasons for the change might be. What was behind it? Why now? He really didn't know, so we brainstormed a few possibilities. We agreed it would be a good thing to find out the reasons behind the changes before charging forward with his assumptions.

The truth is we often make assumptions based on the behaviors of others that may or may not reflect their intentions. That's because we tend to judge others by their behaviors while we judge ourselves based on our intentions. This is human nature.

I next asked Frank what would be the ideal *outcome* to the meeting. As he answered the question, it became clear to him how critical this client was to his company's success and how important it would be to remain on good terms and continue to do business together.

With that understanding, we were able to prepare an outline for a meeting that would lead to the desired result. We crafted some questions that would help Frank understand the impetus for the change and compel his client to understand the impact on Frank's business. We also prepared some comments that would help Frank position the meeting from the start to create a win/win scenario.

Most people go into a meeting like this one without having thought through what they want to accomplish and without creating a plan that will get them where they want to go. Using a framework to guide your thinking can be enormously helpful to obtaining the outcome you want.

Frank was able to turn an emotional situation that could easily have backfired on him into a productive and collaborative conversation with a client that strengthened their overall relationship and increased the level of trust between them. As a result he learned the value of slowing down, thinking through, and being deliberate with his thoughts and actions.

Using a framework for thinking through problems or challenges is so very helpful and effective. It can also be used for thinking through opportunities.

Whenever I discuss taking on a new project with my business coach, she prompts me to ask myself: What is the outcome I want? What's the result I'm looking for? Having that extra bit of *clarity* makes all the difference in achieving success more quickly and efficiently. Additionally, the chances of getting the result I actually want instead of some other result also improve.

As I write this, I realize it may seem obvious. It makes common sense. The thing about common sense is that it is not always common practice. I can't tell you the number of times I've just jumped into something new without thinking it through. When was the last time you did that? And here's the bigger question: what was the outcome?

Let me give you an example of using this approach. Recently I was presented with a business opportunity that on the surface was very exciting. It was flattering when one of my business colleagues singled me out to partner with him on a project that not only played to my strengths but also involved work I love.

When I discussed it with my business coach, she first asked me to think about the ultimate outcome I was looking for in this venture. She urged me to be specific, to play out various scenarios in my mind, and to look at the best case and the worst case. She asked me to consider the time commitment involved and to stack that up against the benefits I would derive, including financial and otherwise. Finally, based on the revenue split proposed for this partnership, we explored the relative value each partner was bringing to the table.

Ultimately, by working through this process, analyzing all potential outcomes, and weighing the options, I realized I was caught up in making an emotional decision that would not serve me well in the long run. I passed on the opportunity, once again truly grateful for the assistance from my business coach. This was a situation that looked like an opportunity I could not pass up and ended up being a trap it would have been difficult to escape.

Having a partner or coach or advisor to help you think things through is an essential resource and an investment I highly recommend. It is one of the things that will really make a difference in your business and your life. As a leader, having a coach will provide you with support and encouragement when you need it, as well as a good kick in the butt when you need that.

Leaders use a framework to support their essential thinking

A framework can be a process. Learning a framework can come from reading a book or attending a workshop or seminar. There are a significant number of books on thinking, and there are also books on any subject you are interested in thinking about.

Workshops and seminars can also be great places to challenge your thinking, but only if you are not a bystander; rather, you participate 100 percent. In other words, pay attention, take notes, take time to reflect on what you learned, determine how you will apply what you learned, and then actually take action.

How consistently do you do all that? How consistently do you participate 100 percent? I know I have a lot of room for improvement here. I love to learn, though I am not as disciplined about putting into action the things I've learned. This is where the real value of learning lives; otherwise it's nothing more than "shelf help."

Taking some practical advice from one of the great thought leaders in your area of expertise can be so very useful. Learn the framework then THINK about how it applies to you and your team, your business, your world. Next, take action on it.

Leaders use a coach, mentor, or critical thinking partner to challenge their thinking

Let's face it. We know that two heads are better than one. The impact is exponentially greater when you add the benefit of someone who has been trained to ask the right questions at the right time. My coach helped me see things from a different perspective that resulted in a better outcome, one that was consistent with my overall business model and strategic direction.

At the peak of his career, Tiger Woods had five or six different coaches. Think about that: the No. 1 golfer in the world at the top of his game needed multiple coaches. Why? Because Tiger can't see his own swing. Neither can you or I.

So whether you are using a framework from a book or one you learned from a thought leader in a workshop or seminar, the important thing here is your willingness to challenge your own thinking. Remember Mindset Must #2: Lead with an open mind and an open heart.

Work past that disempowering "I know" mentality that can shut you down from improving. Or apply something that you already *know* but that you just don't *do*. When you have someone objective and unbiased in your life, they can really help you to break through the "I know."

Being willing to challenge your own thinking or past beliefs allows you to think strategically and gain more clarity. Unless you manage your own thinking, your thoughts end up managing you!

Leaders actually schedule time to think

Scheduling time to think is being proactive and deliberate. One of my teachers and mentors, Keith Cunningham, a successful entrepreneur, author, teacher, and coach, told me this story about Michael Milken. Milken is an ex-con, business magnate, financier, and philanthropist known mostly for his role in the development of the market for junk bonds. He spent two years in prison and paid $200 million in fines and another $400 million in restitution. *Fortune* magazine also called him "The Man Who Changed Medicine" for his extensive funding of medical research.

On this day, Keith was proposing a large business deal to the venture capitalist, with the intention of gaining approval on millions of dollars in funding. Milken was a very busy man and Keith had fifteen minutes to pitch him.

As they were preparing to start, two men walked into the room and asked Milken when he would have an answer for another entrepreneur who had made a pitch earlier. Milken took out his pocket calendar, flipped through it, and said: "The next time I am scheduled to think is 3-5 a.m. on Tuesday. I will have an answer for him on Tuesday morning." So here is a multimillionaire who is prolific in his output, who is involved in multiple business ventures, and whose days are so structured that he actually has to schedule time to think.

You and I may not be operating at the millions of dollars level of venture capitalists like Michael Milken or entrepreneurs like Keith

Cunningham, but let's face it: as you fly through your days, weeks, and months, how much of your time is *not* structured with appointments, tasks, meetings, phone calls, and other commitments?

And within those appointments, how much time do you actually spend being strategic or being thoughtful? And when do you make the best decisions? On the fly? Or after first asking yourself or others some thoughtful questions?

How often do you take time to think—and plan? Being proactive and deliberate by taking 100 percent responsibility for your thinking enables you to lead with intention and to have a bigger impact as a leader.

There are many different ways that really successful people schedule time to quietly review, to plan, and to think. Many companies schedule two days of annual planning, followed by quarterly sessions to review progress, confirm priorities, and schedule execution for the coming quarter. Weekly and daily schedules are used to keep activities on track and assign accountability for outcomes.

Leadership expert John Maxwell enthusiastically shares his annual ritual that occurs the week between Christmas and New Year's Day. He thoroughly reviews his calendar for the year—every appointment, meeting, commitment, and activity, hour by hour—and he evaluates each and every one, asking:

What should I do more of?
What should I do less of?
What should I eliminate altogether?
What growth strategies did I pursue?
What was the return on investment (ROI)?
How much time did I spend on activities that I should delegate in the future?
What activities did I delegate that I should take back?

He evaluates whether he spent enough time with his family. He and his wife even go out to dinner one night and reminisce about the year, thereby enjoying the year's activities all over again.

Why does John do this? It helps him develop strategies for the coming year. Doing this consistently over the years has helped him to be more focused, strategic, and effective each and every year.

I challenge you to try this. Just focus on the last thirty days. Evaluate your activities. How do they align with your current priorities? What should you change? How can you be more effective going forward? This simple practice at the end of each month will help you be more focused, strategic, and effective each and every month.

Brendon Burchard recommends scheduling twenty minutes every single day to think strategically. He believes that most of the things you need to do in your business would actually happen if you sat down and thought strategically, instead of reacting, which is what most of us do.

If it seems to you that twenty minutes is not much time to accomplish something meaningful, I thought the same thing. Then, at one of our Master Mind sessions, Brendon gave us a series of strategic challenges to think through. He asked a specific question and gave us twenty minutes to think and write.

It seemed like a lot to do in a short time, so we were all astonished at how productive just twenty minutes of focused attention, time, and energy could be—and how much we could accomplish.

Using my Simple 5-Step Process for Turning Thoughts into Action, and the questions you will learn in chapter 8, *schedule time* to ask yourself the questions, following the five steps to turn your thinking into inspired, deliberate action. Applying the five simple steps will not only help you to elevate the level of your leadership thinking but also to get the full benefit of it.

Summary: The Habits of Successful Leaders

Creating the *habits of thought* will take you a long way toward greater success as a leader. Thinking strategically as well as tactically will provide better context and improved alignment among your team and throughout your organization. Remembering to identify the outcome you seek will increase your chances of achieving that outcome. Using a framework will provide a process or a way to think through the challenges or opportunities you are facing. Seeking the help of a coach or mentor to challenge you will help you to refine your thinking. And, finally, scheduling time on your calendar to engage in thought will allow you to gain perspective that just isn't possible in the daily crunch of life as we know it.

As we turn our attention to the secret weapon of leaders in the next chapter, you will be in a better position to gain the most benefit from the questions you ask yourself and others.

☞ Usable Insights

- Adopting six critical habits enables a big step forward in becoming deliberate and changing the game of leadership from the inside out:
  1. Thinking with a success mindset
  2. Thinking both strategically and tactically
  3. Using frameworks
  4. Thinking in terms of outcomes
  5. Challenging your thoughts via a critical thinking partner
  6. Scheduling time for thinking
- Developing these habits will help you to manage your own thinking so your thoughts don't end up managing you!

Action Steps

1. Think of a failure you've had or a mistake you've made recently. Make a list of the important lessons that you learned from that experience. Make it a practice to review failures and mistakes this way.

2. Schedule 20 minutes on your calendar in the next week to think about an important issue or question you are facing. Write down whatever comes in to your mind. Do not stop writing or thinking before 20 minutes is up.

Chapter 8

Questions:
The Secret Weapon
of Effective Leaders

Take the attitude of a student. Never be too big to ask questions.
Never know too much to learn something new.
—**Og Mandino**, The Greatest Salesman in the World

Tony Robbins, one of the world leaders in personal transformation and peak-performance strategy, tells us successful people ask better questions, and as a result they get better answers. The quality of the questions we ask—both to others and to ourselves—can make a big difference in the quality of our lives and the information we receive. Asking the right questions is like having the keys to unlock a treasure chest of opportunities.

Most people understand the value of knowledge and education in achieving success in life, but not everyone understands the role *questions* play in this process. Asking better questions will lead to better choices, better decisions, and better actions. Better decisions lead to better results. And those better results will ultimately determine the overall quality of life you enjoy.

When I became a business coach, I learned about the importance of questions in encouraging a client's self-discovery and their willingness to follow through. This is because we are more likely to support that which we create. Giving the answer is never as sustainable as having someone work it out on their own.

Recent breakthroughs in brain research suggest that when a moment of insight occurs, our brains form a complex set of new connections with the potential to rally our mental resources and overcome resistance to change. These insights need to be self-generated, not given, in order to be useful. (*Presence: An Exploration of Profound Change in People, Organizations and Societies,* Peter M. Senge, C. Otto Scharmer, Joseph Jaworski, and Betty Sue Flowers)

> Asking good questions—questions that promote thinking, contemplation, and analysis—will help you help others to make better decisions and reach higher levels of success.

For you as a leader, this means encouraging the introspection and reflection that leads to gaining insights and the so-called "aha!" moments. Asking good questions—questions that promote thinking, contemplation, and analysis—will help you help others to make better decisions and reach higher levels of success.

As you think about the quality of your own life and the results you are getting, what comes to mind? When you think about the quality of your leadership and your results as a leader, are there areas that you would like to improve? Are there ways in which your actions and decisions could improve if you were asking better questions?

Everything starts with the questions you ask yourself. My best teachers, mentors, and coaches all asked the tough questions that challenged my thinking and led to better decisions, more deliberate actions, and improved results.

You can try this now. Think about an area where you want better results. Then simply ask yourself the question: How can I get better results in this area? Determine the actions you need to take and then follow through on those actions. Use the Simple 5-Step Process for Turning Thoughts into Action you learned in chapter 5 to take you from your initial thought or idea all the way to action.

Achieving the quality of life you want can be compromised in many ways. Whenever you are struggling with the results you are getting, consider the actions you are taking and the decisions you are making. Determine where you need to pay more attention or place more focus. Who are your teachers and mentors? And how do they contribute to the quality of your results?

On the other hand, for whom are you a teacher or mentor? And how do you contribute to the people who look up to you? Explore the power of asking yourself better questions as a way to improve your overall results as a leader. Learn how to ask better questions to yourself and to others.

Asking Questions Is a Learning Process

Og Mandino, author of *The Greatest Salesman in the World*, says, "Take the attitude of a student. Never be too big to ask questions. Never know too much to learn something new." Great sales professionals understand the value of asking good questions and asking the right questions.

Can you think of a time you had an experience with a salesperson who assumed he knew exactly what you wanted and what was best for you before learning a single thing about your needs? He just started in, singing the praises of his product or service without even a baseline understanding of your own level of knowledge. The great sales teacher, author, trainer, and coach Jeffrey Gitomer calls this "showing up and throwing up."

On the other hand, how does it feel when an expert sales representative knows enough to ask the two or three key questions that get to the core of your need and then makes a recommendation based on that? It's so helpful! And you're inclined to go along because of the trust that has been established because they cared enough to find out what you need and knew enough to ask the right questions that would lead to the best answer! It's magical when that happens.

Recently I had the experience of purchasing some video equipment. The number of options seemed overwhelming, as did the range of pricing. When I visited my local photo shop, the owner asked me a few key questions regarding my needs and level of experience. Then he made a recommendation based on my answers, and the whole process ended up taking very little time. Not only that, I had confidence in my decision and the result.

By asking the right questions, you too can get a better answer and a better result. This is such a critical skill to develop. It will help you not only in sales, but also in leadership.

And, if you're thinking, "but I'm not *in* sales," think again. Everybody in the world of business is selling something, even if it's just an idea. As a leader, in order to influence others you need to sell them on your ideas and on your vision.

Consider the following questions as unbelievably effective probes to gain important information and knowledge:

The Simple, Most Powerful Question

Perhaps the simplest, most powerful question to ask yourself is: **What do I want?**

If you're like me, and a lot of other people I know, this may be a difficult question to answer. If that's the case, simply ask yourself: **What is it I don't want?** Sometimes that second question is much easier to answer than the first. Sometimes we just don't know what we want but we are confident in what we don't want.

Actually, I used to have a lot of trouble with this question myself. My attention was so centered on what others wanted (so I could meet their needs) that I never really took the time to figure out what I wanted. I didn't realize it at the time, but this led to a life by accident and not by design. Many women have this same problem. In fact, they often struggle with this more than men do. The most likely explanation is based on their traditional role as caregivers in the family. They see to everyone else's needs but their own, which inevitably leads to living an unfulfilling life.

My meditation teacher Laura said, "You can't give away what you don't have." I've heard others say this as well, and it reminds me of the advice flight attendants give when you're sitting in your seat about to take off: "Place your own oxygen mask on first before assisting other passengers."

How many women have you known who experienced complete burnout from caring for their kids, spouses, parents, as well as customers and team members and other constituents in their business or careers? Taking good care of yourself—physically, mentally, emotionally, and spiritually—is enormously important to avoid this travesty. It allows you to be in the best possible condition to help others and provides stress resiliency when the going gets tough.

It is an understatement to say that "what do I want?" and "what is it I don't want?" are loaded questions. These two simple but valuable questions can really help you gain clarity about the outcome you are looking for. Your chances of obtaining your desired outcome increase when you have clarity. This level of clarity is one of the great gifts in working with a trained coach. And while I recommend having a coach— or more than one—you can also function as your own coach when you ask questions like this.

But what if you are stuck with this question? My response: **"Well, if I did know, what would it be?"** This may seem flippant or silly, but it works. A great exercise is to write down these questions or to make two columns on a page titled "want/don't want" and write down things you want to have, to do, or to be. Keep this list somewhere handy where you can add to it. And rest assured you are not alone.

Lou Holtz, former head football coach at Notre Dame and several other college teams, strongly believes in this practice. When Holtz was twenty-eight years old and out of a job with a child on the way, his wife, hoping to boost his spirits, gave him a copy of David Schwartz's *The Magic of Thinking Big*. Schwartz encouraged him to make a list of the things he wanted or dreamed of having in his life.

Holtz made a list of 107 things that included:

- Having dinner at the White House
- Appearing on *The Tonight Show* with Johnny Carson
- Meeting the pope
- Shooting a hole in one
- Coaching Notre Dame
- Winning a national championship

The rest is history. He achieved all of these and more. But here is where it gets interesting. When he was getting close to accomplishing all those, he made another list, knowing that striving for success is a lifelong journey. This is the power of being deliberate and intentional in our thinking. We are all capable of achieving a great deal more than we think!

The important thing is you don't need to know *how* you will "have, do, or be" the things on that list when you write them. Just the act of creating clarity and writing them down will put your subconscious to work on the how.

One of the reasons this simple question is one of my all-time favorites is because it can be used many different ways. This can be a very strategic question to help you think through a major initiative or change. You can use it in your strategic planning process to identify goals, key targets, and priorities. You can ask it to yourself—and to others.

Try this with either a problem or challenge you are currently facing, or with an opportunity you are considering. Ask yourself: What do I want, and what is it I don't want?

As a leader, it can help you to better understand what's important to your team members, your boss, your colleagues, and your customers. You can even use it to figure out where to go and what to do on your vacation!

Simple, powerful questions

- What do I want?
- What is it I don't want?
- What kind of leader do I want to be?
- What do I have to do?
- Who do I have to become?
- How will I define success?
- What will be my core values and guiding principles?

Questions to Improve Leadership Ability and Credibility

The next question to ask yourself is: **What kind of leader do I want to be?** You can substitute the word "leader" for any other role here as you are trying to decide who you want to be, how you want to be, and how you want to be perceived by others. For example, you may want to ask yourself: What kind of parent or what kind of friend do I want to be?

There are a series of other questions that help take this inquiry to a deeper level. For example:

What do I have to **do** to be that kind of leader? In other words, what are the **actions** people need to **see** from me in order to be seen as the kind of leader I want to **be**?

Who do I have to **become** to be that kind of leader? In other words, how do I have to be thinking in order to do the things I need to do to be seen as the type of leader I want to be?

For example, if you want to be thought of as a *caring leader*, one who cares about your team, ask yourself, what specific *actions* do people need to see from me? And, very importantly, in order to be perceived as a caring leader, a caring person, you have to think like a caring person thinks.

Think about who you have to **become**. How do you have to start **thinking**? You may need to become more present, more focused, more "in the moment." You may need to become curious, more interested, and perhaps less self-absorbed. You need to be **thinking** about the other person and not about yourself.

Questions like "what do I have to do?" and "who do I have to become?" and "how do I need to think?" are questions of **intention**. They also lead to answers that will help you gain **clarity** about a course of **action**. They will help you to be more **deliberate** as a leader.

But remember it always starts with **awareness.**

Awareness always comes first. Once you have awareness on the type of leader you want to be, how you want to be seen, what you need to do, and how you need to think, you can begin to track your own performance against those qualities, traits, and behaviors. And you can assess how you are doing.

You can use the simple steps of sharing it, testing it, and asking for feedback. When you are able to get perspectives from others about your progress, this leads to improvement. This leads to better results.

Doctor Paul, the People-Pleaser

Paul is a doctor and the managing partner in his practice, with three other doctors. When we first started working together, Paul admitted that he was a good doctor who knew nothing about running a business.

From our early conversations, I observed that Paul was intimidated by the idea of "managing" his peers. He was a natural people-pleaser. He liked things to be smooth, consistent, stable, and harmonious. He disliked confrontation, and he was concerned about hurting people's feelings.

In theory, these are all great qualities. However, in the context of leading the team, these behaviors were serving neither Paul nor the practice. As we talked through this, he clearly saw the issue. He would wait till things got beyond untenable before addressing them, and then he would make himself sick with worry about the outcome.

So we went to work on how Paul thinks. He gained a level of awareness and clarity of intention when he was able to describe the type of leader he wanted to be and how he wanted to be perceived by the rest of his peers. With a deeper understanding of his preferences and natural tendencies, he was better able to overcome the things that were getting in his way.

We often talked through specific scenarios so that he could prepare to have difficult conversations with his colleagues. We would determine the outcome he wanted. We would consider how his team members might view the situation and what possible reactions they might have.

With awareness, intention, and clarity about the outcome he wanted, Paul was able to formulate a plan of action. He knew what he had to do. He knew what he had to say. He knew where he needed to end up and so if things got off track he could find his way back.

Over time he gained the ability and confidence to walk himself through the process. Today Paul operates on a whole different level as a leader. He has more confidence. The practice is growing. His team is flourishing. He's getting better results and that is leading to a better quality of life for Paul and his family, and a better quality of life for the rest of the doctors in the practice.

Whenever Paul wants to expand, he has no trouble finding new doctors to join the practice because of his leadership ability. People want to work with him.

Paul did the hard inside work of becoming a better leader, and he learned to ask better questions—to his colleagues and to himself. That, my friends, is the power of questions.

Defining Success as a Leader

Asking **"How will I define success as a leader?"** is another way to gain clarity of intention and clarity of outcome or result. Being clear about how you will define your success allows you to better measure your success and your progress.

Remembering that leadership development is a lifelong pursuit, it's important to recognize how you are doing along the way. You can ask this question to provide overall direction and also with respect to a particular set of circumstances or a specific situation or even a particular person. In any case, understanding how you will define success is extremely helpful to achieving it.

A series of questions will help you answer one big question: **How will I lead?** These questions will help you determine the kind of leader you will be and how you will be seen by others. Giving thought to how you intend to handle some of your responsibilities as a leader will also illuminate your strengths, the areas where you need to improve, and help you to set priorities for your development. For example:

How and when will you communicate?
How will you make decisions?
How will you handle conflict?
How will you set vision and gain alignment?
How will you set and manage expectations?
How will you provide feedback?
What will you do to inspire your team?

Defining Personal Success

Another important question that can drive your overall approach to leadership is: **"What are my personal core values and the guiding principles I will live by and lead by?"** Answering this question will help you build a strong foundation as a leader. In chapter 7 we explored the habits of successful leaders, including thinking on both strategic and tactical levels. Identifying core values enables you to do that.

Answering questions about your envisioned future, your vision, and your core purpose will guide your behavior, your decisions, and the actions you take on a macro and micro level. In other words, you can use this series of questions to guide your life or to define a specific project or task.

What are those guiding principles that you hold near and dear no matter where you are, where you go, and who you lead? Or, what are the guiding principles you will use to work through a particular situation today that will ensure you get the outcome you want?

Defining core values is one of the most valuable things you can determine for yourself, your business, your team, and even for your family. If you already have a set of core values, be sure to revisit it on a regular basis to see if it is aligning with where you are now and where you are headed.

You may work for or own a company that has core values and guiding principles as well. If so, you may need to examine the extent to which your personal values align with those of the organization. When that happens, it is so much easier to gain credibility and build trust. When it doesn't, it's so much harder to gain any traction at all.

It is powerful beyond words when your behavior matches and actually demonstrates the values you intend. Leaders, after all, are role models, whether or not they choose to be. People pay more attention to your actions and behaviors than they do to your words. When you are able to recognize yourself for who you are—warts and all—you are better able to build your self-acceptance, self-respect, and self-esteem. It's a great starting point for realizing that we are all works in progress and that room for improvement is the biggest room in the house.

Defining Development Needs

As we continue along our journey through asking crucial questions to identify vital answers, consider the following: **What skills, knowledge, and abilities do I need to develop?** This can be a lot to think about. In fact, it can be positively overwhelming, so let's chunk it down.

To start, a great question to consider is: **What is the one thing that, if I were better at it, would make a big difference in my business or career?**

If you've ever used a leadership assessment tool, you may have identified areas that you need to focus on to be more effective. In my work, I use a variety of assessment tools with my clients. Each has its best purpose and use, and all can be extremely valuable in getting to know—and accept—your authentic self.

These tools can really facilitate your self-improvement initiatives by helping you to focus on the development needs that will make the biggest possible impact on your results.

Along with your own leadership development, you may be responsible for those you lead—beyond yourself. It's a good idea to think about the needs of your team:

What skills, knowledge, and abilities do you want to develop in others?

How will you do that?

How will you prepare yourself and your team for future challenges?

The use of assessment tools can be helpful here as well. By analyzing strengths, weaknesses, opportunities, and threats for your business and your team members, you can use this information to set some priorities for the development needs of specific individuals or the entire team.

There may be specific **strengths** you want to build on or spread to other team members, and there may be **weaknesses** that clarify a specific training need. For example, maybe you only have one team member skilled at handling customer problems and you want everyone to improve that trait. Your response may be to create an action plan based on your team member's behaviors and skill set to train the rest of the team.

Or maybe you feel that leadership skills are lacking in your organization, and you want to build the leadership capability and effectiveness of your team. In response, you may plan to enroll people in a leadership and development program or to bring in an expert to train and coach the team on leadership.

Considering both **opportunities** that you'd like to leverage and **threats** that exist in your current environment may also lead you to some training or development needs for yourself, your team, and your organization.

For example, there may be an *opportunity* to use social media to grow your business and reach out to new potential communities of customers. In order to do that, you need to learn the ins and outs of social media to decide which will work best for you and then create a strategy that supports your goals in this area.

Or perhaps there is a *threat* in the form of legal or regulatory changes that will affect your business, and you need to get yourself and the rest of the team up to speed in order to get in front of those developments and meet that threat head-on.

When you are deliberate and thoughtful about your own professional growth, and that of your team, your ROI in training and skill development increases dramatically. Many critical leadership capabilities are sometimes referred to as "soft skills." But in reality they are the needle movers when it comes to leading with impact and intention.

When you work to grow these you are improving as a leader, and your ability to connect and influence is increasing, leading to bigger and better results.

Ask yourself what you and your team can do to specifically improve in these areas:

- Building and managing relationships
- Developing trust
- Improving your credibility
- Modeling behavior
- Communicating with clarity
- Listening empathically
- Inspiring people
- Having fun
- Improving life overall

Asking these questions and working through the Simple 5-Step Process for Turning Thoughts into Action: writing it down, sharing and testing it, getting feedback, and implementing it leads you from thoughts and ideas to action. Be crystal clear on the outcome you want and how you will measure your success. Then, and only then, will you find yourself better positioned to ask the questions that give rise to the answers you need to improve, grow, and flourish as a leader.

☞ Usable Insights

- Learning to ask better questions encourages introspection and reflection, promotes greater insight and results in better choices and better outcomes.

- Questions facilitate both strategic and tactical thinking. They raise awareness and bring clarity. The right questions simplify the complex.

- Leaders improve their ability and credibility by asking impactful questions to others. Effective questioning helps define personal and professional success by identifying strengths and opportunities, as well as priorities.

- Using questions in conjunction with the Simple 5-Step Process for Turning Thoughts into Action will lead to better results.

👣 Action Steps

1. Next time a team member approaches you with a problem ask, "What do you want?" Help them to define the specific outcome they seek and determine the steps to get to that outcome.

2. Make a 20-minute appointment on your calendar each week and journal your thoughts about each of the questions in this chapter, one at a time, starting at the beginning and working all the way through.

Chapter 9

Flip the Switch:

Deactivating the Power
of Negative Thoughts

*You are today where your thoughts have brought you; you will be
tomorrow where your thoughts take you.*
—James Allen

S tudies show the average person talks to himself about seventy-
eighty thousand times per day. Most of that "self-talk" is
often critical and negative. This can be extremely dangerous
as thoughts certainly affect your attitude, your physiology, and your
motivation to act. Your negative thoughts can actually control your
behavior and create changes in your heart rate, blood pressure, muscle
tension, and breathing.

Frankly, your thoughts can empower or disempower you, uplift you or keep you down. So learning to identify your automatic negative thinking and replace it with more positive, affirming thinking can ultimately alter the direction of your life. The impact is simply magical once you realize you are solely in charge of whether or not to listen or agree with your thoughts.

So let's focus our energy on positive thinking. There are several simple yet powerful ways of turning negative thinking around, and in this chapter we will discuss them so you can implement them into your life and the lives of those you lead.

> Your vision for what you can achieve should not be limited by your current knowledge and capabilities.
>
> *–Brendon Burchard*
>
> Nor should it be limited by someone else's concept of what those are.
>
> *–Cheryl Bonini Ellis*

How often do you tell yourself "great job!" or "well done!" or "you're awesome"? Or are you like most people where the majority of what you say *to* yourself *about* yourself when you are *by* yourself is negative or falls into the category of "beating yourself up"?

Your thoughts literally create physiological reactions, and your body can't tell the difference between what's real and what is vividly imagined. That means your thoughts are far more powerful than you may even realize. Your limiting beliefs and negative thoughts can be harmful and detrimental to your life outcomes.

In a workshop I attended, I had a profound experience that demonstrates the power of visualization. We were asked to stand and close our eyes while we were guided through a vivid, detailed description of standing at the very edge on top of a giant skyscraper. Most people, including me, had an intense physical reaction to this activity as if we were actually experiencing the situation for real. Afterwards, as we described our fears, we were amazed at how realistic it felt. We had totally responded to the vision in our own minds!

Olympic athletes employ the practice of visualization to enhance their performance by using their imaginations to change their thoughts and expectations. Actors and other celebrities have also used creative visualization to overcome challenges and envision their successes long before they actually achieved them. So why can't you?

Common Negative Thought Patterns

Automatic Negative Thoughts

Dr. Daniel Amen is a clinical neuroscientist, psychiatrist, and brain-imaging expert, founder of the world-renowned Amen Clinics, author of many books, and producer of several PBS shows on the brain. In his work, he introduces the subject of ANTs—Automatic Negative Thoughts—and how they can ruin your experience of life.

There are many different types of negative thoughts, and it is important for you as a leader to learn how to become aware of negative thoughts, challenge them, and then replace them with more positive, affirming ones.

Consider some of the most common negative thoughts we all cope with:

1. Self-pity coupled with "always" or "never" thinking
2. Guilt and/or resentment toward others
3. Limiting beliefs with no real basis in truth
4. Blame, excuses, and denial
5. Worry and fear about things over which we have no control

Other forms of negative thinking include perspectives like seeing what's wrong with the situation rather than what's right, projecting a negative outcome, and assigning motives to others without knowing their real intentions. These are just a few examples of how we sabotage our thoughts through negative thinking.

How often have you labeled yourself or someone else with words like stupid, idiot, dummy, ugly, fat, or lazy? And here's one especially for women: count how many times during the course of a day that you hear yourself or other women say "I'm sorry." It's not only a negative description, it's self-deprecating and self-defeating, leading to poor self-esteem and even poorer results.

Raising your awareness of how often your mind automatically drifts to these kinds of thoughts is a powerful first step toward overcoming them and deactivating the power they have over you.

The Guilty Imposter

During one of my leadership retreats for women of influence, we were doing an activity designed to help participants work through feelings of guilt. One woman—let's call her Jackie—was really struggling with this task.

Jackie had started a nonprofit organization because of her passion for helping at-risk and underprivileged teenage girls. She was offering programs for teenage girls to help build their self-esteem, to teach them to set goals, and to learn how to think independently so they could be accountable and responsible leaders. Jackie was having a major impact on these girls, who were at critical crossroads in their lives and in great need of her guidance.

However, Jackie felt like an imposter. Early in her own life, she had not always made great choices while facing her own critical challenges and some serious abuse. And, although she learned to forgive those who hurt her, she had not fully forgiven herself.

Now she was wondering "who am I to help these girls—to guide them, advise them, and mentor them—when I haven't fully dealt with my own junk?" Jackie was carrying some very heavy baggage!

From her self-imposed negative perspective, she didn't really see how her own experience not only gave her complete insight and empathy to what these girls felt, but also was actually the very basis for her credibility in helping them. Jackie had allowed the negative voices in her head to completely drown out her own self-esteem, her own self-confidence, and even her conviction that she was doing the right thing. She seriously doubted herself and her mission.

Together we did an activity that involved Jackie holding a conversation out loud with the two competing voices in her head—the encouraging one that said she was doing the best she could and the critical one that challenged her with "just who do you think you are?" and "who are you kidding?" The effect was immediate, dramatic, and emotional.

It had a powerful impact on her to accept that she could overcome those negative thoughts and replace them with positive, constructive, and encouraging thoughts.

More importantly, it improved her ability to connect with and influence the young women she mentored. These girls felt fully empowered. Jackie is a wonderful role model to these young women, and she is really making a difference in the world.

Most people experience those negative voices, and yet they don't realize they have a choice about whether or not to listen. You do have a choice and can learn how to replace the negative voices with positive, empowering ones.

Learning to Reject the Negative Voices

According to James Allen, author of *As A Man Thinketh*, "you are today where your thoughts have brought you; you will be tomorrow where your thoughts take you." Think about the impact of rejecting the negative voices in your head and replacing them with powerful, positive voices as Jackie did. What if you could learn to talk to yourself with kindness and love and encouragement instead of disapproval and criticism?

Imagine transforming your negative self-talk into positive self-talk while silencing your thoughts of limitation and replacing them with thoughts of unmitigated possibility. It can transform your life when you are able to replace thinking like a victim with thinking like an influential, powerful leader. And when you are able to model that behavior and thinking for others, you possess the power and influence to transform their lives!

> *You* are ultimately in charge of whether or not to listen to or agree with any thought.

You can learn how to replace your inner critic who judges your every move with a supportive inner coach who will encourage you and give you confidence as you face new situations and challenges. All it takes is a little awareness, focus, and intention. The key is to realize that *you* are ultimately in charge of whether or not to **listen to** or **agree with** any thought. In other words, just because you think it or hear it doesn't mean it's true. Here are six practices that will help you overcome negative thinking.

6 Practices to Overcome Negative Thinking

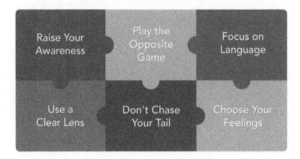

1. **Awareness**. The first practice is to become more aware. To raise your awareness, try this for several days: tune in to every negative thought you think or say out loud, and any you hear anyone else say. Keep track by writing them down, and then conduct a reality check, looking for tangible evidence to support your thinking. Ask yourself:
   - Is this thought helping me or hurting me?
   - Is it moving me closer to, or further away from, where I want to go?
   - Is it motivating me to take action, or is it preventing me by filling me with fear and self-doubt?

2. **Play the Opposite Game**. Another practice is to consider the opposite of the original thought. For example, you can train yourself to become more optimistic by looking for the positive

in any negative situation. Or, by recognizing that few things in life are absolute—always or never—you can stop yourself from turning a temporary situation into a permanent reality or limiting belief.

3. **Focus on Your Language**. Practice paying special attention to your language. Using words like "should" and "have to" create guilt, resentment, and internal resistance. You automatically empower yourself when you replace these words with "choose to." Guilt is hardly ever productive and often leads to bad choices. Letting go of guilt and reclaiming your power of choice allows you to focus on what you can control.

> Letting go of guilt and reclaiming your power of choice allows you to focus on what you can control.

4. **Use a Clear Lens.** Practice examining your feelings with a clear lens. Sometimes feelings lie, especially when you are over-tired, stressed out, or worried. Stepping back from the situation or even sleeping on it can provide an entirely different perspective. Using part of the Simple 5-Step Process for Turning Thoughts into Action (write it down, share it, test it, get feedback) will also help clarify your thoughts and feelings.

5. **Don't Chase Your Tail.** Understand that you never really know why other people do what they do. Trying to is like chasing your tail. Ask yourself: Do I *know* they feel that way? Am I *certain* I know the reason they did what they did? And just *how* do I know it for sure? Practice resisting the urge to assign motives to another's behavior.

6. **Choose Your Feelings.** Remember that where you focus your attention determines how you feel. One of my favorite examples

on this point involves my friend JJ Virgin. JJ is the bestselling author of *The Virgin Diet* and one of the nation's foremost nutrition and fitness experts.

Several years ago, just as the launch of her book and a national publicity tour was scheduled, JJ's son Grant nearly lost his life when he was hit by a car while walking home. In fact, at one point he was given a 5 percent chance of survival and his parents were encouraged to "let him go."

JJ's steadfast focus was on Grant's survival, healing, and rehabilitation, and she fought off any effort by others to engage her thinking about finding the hit-and-run driver, getting revenge, or giving up hope of Grant's full recovery. She posted updates on Facebook regularly and received encouragement and support from her friends and fans and complete strangers, all of which reinforced her own determination to focus on Grant's improvement.

Grant's recovery was miraculous, and I'm convinced that JJ's positive attitude and thinking were major contributors to getting JJ and her family through this unthinkable challenge. Throughout her ordeal, JJ never compromised her own health and fitness regimen, making whatever accommodations were necessary to keep herself strong, healthy, and resilient.

Living in a Heaven or Hell of Our Own Making

Byron Katie, author of *Loving What Is: Four Questions That Can Change Your Life*, teaches a method of self-inquiry known simply as The Work. It is a way to identify and question the stressful thoughts that cause pain and suffering, then to create a turnaround, which is a way to experience the opposite of your belief.

Katie's insight is that it is not life or other people that make us feel depressed, angry, stressed, abandoned, or despairing. It is our own thoughts that make us feel that way. In other words, we can live in a hell of our own making or we can live in a heaven of our own creation.

This vantage point will make a big impact on how you think and how you model thinking for others. It is especially helpful when your thoughts involve judging others, or in those cases when you are torturing yourself by assigning motives to the behaviors of others.

Here is how it works. First you identify the stressful thought and ask:

1. Is it true?
2. Can I absolutely know that it's true?
3. How do I react when I believe that thought?
4. Who would I be—or how would I feel—without the thought?

Next, you create the turnaround, a "what if" scenario, by taking the opposite of your original thought and asking whether it's truer than the original thought.

For example, let's say you're convinced that one of your coworkers is "out to get me." As a result of that thinking, every interaction you have with that person seems to reinforce your belief. So you ask yourself:

1. Is this particular thought true? Yes, I think so.
2. Can I absolutely know that it's true? Well, I can't say **absolutely**.
3. How do I react when I believe that thought? I feel tense and defensive. I'm expecting the worst and feeling like I have to protect myself. As a kind of preemptive strike, I might even badmouth her to others.
4. Who would I be—or how would I feel—without the thought? I would feel more relaxed and confident about my work situation. I'd probably be more productive and more positive. I'd be happier here.

Now for the turnaround: **What if** your coworker wants to help you, support you, and work collaboratively with you? Do you *know* that's not true? *Could* it be truer than your belief that she *is* out to get you? In this case, you say "I will decide to behave as if she wants to be helpful and supportive, and I will reach out to be helpful and supportive to her, because that's the kind of relationship and work situation that I want."

Questioning your thoughts helps you to understand they are *only thoughts, not reality*. Try this today with something or someone you are struggling with. Write down your thoughts, answer the questions, do the turnaround.

Is Self-Judgment Motivated by Love?

When you were a little kid, did your parents ever yell at you or send you to your room for doing something "stupid" like playing with matches? Maybe you've done this with your own kids.

We all know the real message here is: "I love you. I don't want you to get burned. I want you to stay safe so that I can enjoy watching you grow up into a happy healthy adult."

Instead, what is said is something like this: "What's wrong with you? Were you born without a brain? Playing with matches is dangerous! You could have burned the whole house down! You should know better. Go to your room and think about what you just did."

The expression is one of anger alone, while underneath the anger are three more parts to the message that never got delivered: fear, specific requests, and love. Here's how this might sound when all the parts are expressed.

Anger: I am mad at you for playing with matches.

Fear: I am afraid that you are going to get badly burned.

Requests: I want you to understand that type of playing can be dangerous to you, and I want you to play safely.

Love: I love you so much. I don't know what I'd do without you. You are precious to me. I want you to be safe and healthy. You deserve to have fun and stay safe so you can enjoy life to the fullest. Do you understand?

Sounds like a different message, doesn't it? **What if you learned to talk to yourself that way?** What if you realized that self-judgment and self-criticism are really just acts of self-care and self love?

Here's how you can use this: you can write it out on paper or you can have an actual conversation out loud with yourself. In a workshop, I have had people set two chairs facing each other and move from one chair to another to carry on the conversation. In fact, an activity like this one is what led Jackie to her amazing breakthrough, which also had a compelling impact on everyone else in the room as they witnessed the transformation.

Whenever you find yourself judging yourself, you can simply reply: "Thanks for caring." Then ask, "What is your fear? What specifically do you want me to do? How will this serve me? Thank you."

If instead you continue to listen to that negative voice, it can undermine your self-confidence, lower your self-esteem, and become truly demoralizing.

The inner critic becomes an inner coach that is simply pointing out ways to improve future results when you decide to tell the inner voice that you are not willing to listen to any more character assassinations, name-calling, or brow-beating—only specific action steps you can take to do it better the next time.

There are a lot of things your inner coach observes about how to improve your performance in future situations. The problem is when it presents the information as a judgment. The experience changes from a negative to a positive one once you switch the conversation to a non-emotional discussion of improvement opportunities.

All of the methods described in this chapter can help you overcome your negative thinking. Overcoming your negative thinking will make a huge difference in your life, in your leadership, in your level of influence, and ultimately in your results.

Taking control of your thoughts is a choice, and once you make the choice, you have to work at it. You have to be deliberate and intentional, and over time it will become your default reaction and habitual behavior. Once your habits are shaped and formed as positive ones, you will quickly find substantial and positive changes within your life. Things will start falling your way. Your prior failures will become your future successes. And your life will begin to align with your hopes for it. Taking control of your thoughts will be worth the effort.

☞ Usable Insights

- Thoughts can be powerful enablers or disablers. Learn to focus your energy on positive thinking.

- Most of us engage in automatic negative thinking much of the time and we don't always realize that we have the ability to choose our thoughts, much the way we can choose our attitudes or behaviors.

- There are several common patterns of negative thinking. Once you realize that *you* are ultimately in charge of whether or not to listen to or agree with any thought, you can take steps to change the default patterns.

- Like other habits, learning to practice positive thinking over negative thinking takes time and effort and attention. Modeling these habits for others will contribute to their overall well-being and success and your impact as a leader.

Action Steps

1. For one week, practice awareness by tuning in to your thoughts and language and the language you hear from others. Notice how often they are negative and make a conscious effort to replace them with positive thoughts and words. Journal your observations.

2. Think of a difficult relationship you have that you would like to improve. Identify instances when you are assigning motives to that other person. Imagine the opposite were true and act toward the person with that new belief. Note what happens.

Chapter 10

Being the Difference:

Applying the Lessons
of Leadership

*Thinking is the hardest work there is, which is probably the reason
so few engage in it.*

—Henry Ford

Find a reason to celebrate life every day: Live. Love. Learn. Laugh. As we conclude this book, there are few lessons I can impart more crucial and valuable than that one. During the writing of this book, my best friend and the love of my life was diagnosed with a rare form of bladder cancer. As you can imagine, it was devastating to us both. Optimistic by nature, we worked through the protocol of medical tests and procedures together, hoping for positive results each step of the way. We quickly learned that isolating the source and nature of such a cancer would be both a long and frustrating process. This tested my impatient nature to its limits. I learned to take one step at a time and have faith in the process and in the professional expertise of the doctors who trained throughout their lives to address these situations. Ultimately I learned to honor the journey and to identify the valuable lessons that emerged.

On the advice of our urologist, we sought a second opinion at the world-renowned Memorial Sloan Kettering Cancer Center. Following a surgical procedure to scope the area and gather more cells for examination, as I sat by his side in recovery, I noticed just how special the quality of care was. Doctors, nurses, and orderlies alike were professional, competent, and confident in their movements, yet compassionate and interested in both the patient's and the caretaker's well-being. They patiently listened to stories, answered questions they had heard thousands of times, and made us feel we had their undivided attention.

I asked several of the nurses how long they had worked there and how they felt about being there. It was clear that these are coveted jobs for anyone who wants to work with cancer patients. They all seemed to feel completely at home, like they were doing what they wanted, where they wanted, and how they wanted. As a lifelong student of human and organizational behavior and culture, I could feel the positive energy of a healthy, happy work environment. And as a lifelong student of leadership excellence, I realize that this type of culture starts at the very top of the organization and is built on every level with attention and intention. This does not happen by accident. Institutions like Sloan Kettering are a product of those who lead them.

You Need to Have a Good Soul

One nurse described it this way: "In order to work here, you need to have a good soul. Not everyone has a good soul, you know. If you don't have a good soul, you cannot last here. You stand out like a sore thumb, and then you leave." As I reflected on that conversation and what it means to have a "good soul," it occurred to me that great leadership requires a good soul. To be a better leader, you must learn to be a better person. All strong, authentic leadership emanates from who you are on the inside.

> "In order to work here, you need to have a good soul. Not everyone has a good soul, you know. If you don't have a good soul, you cannot last here. You stand out like a sore thumb, and then you leave."
>
> —Nurse at Sloan Kettering

Doing the tough inside work of leadership is essential to becoming the best person and the best leader you can be. Leaders are born, but the qualities that make you a great leader are developed over the course of your life. It is always a work in progress, and it is a lifelong process. As a nurse at Sloan Kettering, having a good soul means being totally focused on the patient and doing your best work to make that patient feel cared for, cared about, and confident that he or she is in the very best hands the medical industry can offer. It means being attentive to the details your professional training requires and at the same time being attuned to the physical, emotional, mental, and spiritual needs of the patient.

As a leader, having a good soul also means being focused on others. It means that your motivation should be intrinsic rather than extrinsic. In other words, it needs to come from a place deep inside your core that reflects your values and purest intentions. It needs to capture who you are as a person relative to other people. It is easier to make the lifelong commitment it takes to being a better leader when you truly desire to help make other people's lives better, to make them more effective, more productive, more confident, as well as happier, healthier, and wealthier.

Desire Alone Is Not Enough

The only way to effect true lasting change is to commit to it and make it a "nonnegotiable." It has to be a "must do," not a "nice to do." The distinguishing factor between desire and commitment is the willingness and ability to take action. Making that level of *commitment* to do the tough inside work of leadership requires a big enough "why." You are better able to overcome resistance when you have a big enough why. You are willing to act even when you feel unwilling. You are able to push forward past your fears and doubts.

The lasting formula for success lies in knowing what that "why" is for you, understanding its power to propel you forward, committing to whatever it takes, and then taking those actions one step at a time. It requires holding the vision, the intention, and understanding how it all relates to your core values. It requires true commitment.

Your level of commitment and resolve will be tested again and again on the path to more effective leadership. You will have doubts. You will have fears. You will have questions about your ability to even lead. You will face crises of confidence. You will ask whether you have what it takes. You may even feel conflicted. At those times, you must reach deep down inside to that core of desire and to the reason it is there. I cannot tell you what that "why" is for you. But I can tell you that it is worth knowing and it is worth the effort to figure it out. Don't be surprised if it takes some time.

Set your intention and head in the direction that seems right. The answers will be revealed sometime and somewhere along the way. And it may not be until you face the biggest obstacles, the most difficult tests, the toughest problems, and the most demanding challenges that you realize what you are truly made of.

For me, the challenge came with that diagnosis. As we drove home and he asked me, "As I go through this process, what do you think my mindset should be?" I realized that I would be tested beyond my experience to date. I remember thinking *that which doesn't kill us makes us stronger* and resolving that we would get through this. I recognized that it would take every bit of strength, courage, and positive energy I could muster. I understood that I needed to model the behavior of confidence and certainty that everything would be all right.

I was speaking as much for myself as to him when I answered: "I would set my sights on the outcome that I want, and I would hold that vision with intention. And whenever I had fears or doubts about that outcome, I would gently acknowledge them as human and then move them aside, replacing them with more positive, uplifting thinking. And I would focus my attention on those happier, healthier thoughts. Finally, I would remind myself—as often as necessary—that I am not in this battle alone, and when it gets tough I am willing and able to lean on the love and support of others." Looking at him, I added: "And I will be with you every step of the way."

That answer came from deep inside my spirit. I did not think about it first, it just came out of me. If you're paying attention, each and every experience you have in life will contribute to the leader you become—to the person you are. And you will be prepared when your time comes. If you have been doing the tough inside work of leadership, the courage, strength, and confidence you need is there for you when you need it.

The power plant doesn't *have* energy, the power plant *generates* energy.

—Brendon Purchard

As Brendon Burchard reminds us, "The power plant doesn't *have energy*, the power plant *generates energy*." And if you have been working on you, you will be able to generate what you need in the moment—whether it be energy, courage, strength, or confidence.

In retrospect, I realize that all the tough inside work I've been doing for years has enabled me to lead myself and my dearest patient through this journey. Taking good care of your physical, emotional, mental, and spiritual well-being will help you build up an incredible store of stress resilience, just like my friend JJ Virgin. Friends and family alike have commented on my level of composure, my positive attitude, and my ability to maintain a sense of humor. You too can behave with grace under pressure if you have been working on you!

When you practice taking 100 percent responsibility for your life, you are able to quickly work through, over, or around the challenges you will inevitably face. When these seem to be coming at you from every direction, as they are for me right now, taking ownership and accountability for the part you *can* control—you and only you—helps you to accept that some things are outside your control. Accepting that and letting those things go can be liberating. Avoiding the urge to make excuses or to blame others allows you to focus on the solution and take action toward that, instead of wasting valuable time and energy.

Learning to choose your thoughts so that your thinking doesn't control you leads to a *habit* of expecting the best possible outcome.

In the beginning, it may be necessary to remind yourself that you always have a choice. And the power to choose is enormous.

For example, you can choose to believe. And what you truly believe is more likely to occur. By setting aside your own doubts and fears, you can focus on what you need to do to be effective and productive.

My lifelong practice of doing the inside work of leadership has enabled me in so many ways to face my current challenges. This practice will continue forever, and I am excited about that. Because I still have more work to do. I am still learning not to judge myself so harshly. I am still learning to let go of that which does not serve me. I am still learning to honor my own internal voice. I am still learning to lead with an open mind and an open heart. I am still—and always will be—a work in progress.

As you undertake—or continue—to do the tough inside work of leadership, you will always find more work to do too. Yours may be like mine or it may be different. Learn to honor the journey, including the inevitable struggles and challenges from which you will gain many benefits.

Remember that when you improve, everything around you improves. Your business improves and so does your life. Your outlook and attitude improve. Your relationships improve. Both your results and the overall quality of your life improve.

> Leading yourself allows you to lead others.

And there lies the most important message my journey and this book have to offer. Leading yourself allows you to lead others. Who knows when? Who really knows where? Who knows how? Only the journey will present the answers to these important questions. But when you work to become a great leader and further position yourself to be that leader, you will find that the opportunity eventually presents itself. I never expected to stand where I do today. But I also recognize that all the work I did internally allows me to resonate and glow with the external strength my husband needs from me today.

So as you close this book and move through your own unique and special journey, do so with the knowledge and wisdom that life will call you to lead. It may not be today, or even tomorrow, but at some point you will be gifted with the opportunity to improve and bear the weight of the life of another. And if you are prepared, you can truly be the difference that person needs.

Having more influence will enable you to have a bigger impact and to make a greater difference in your world and in *the* world. When you are able to do that, it's a gift that adds meaning and purpose to your life. It makes you feel more significant, knowing that you matter. You **do** matter, because you are a role model to others. Your role is to bring awareness, acceptance, and accountability—all while inspiring action. That's both a privilege and a responsibility. It's also a huge opportunity. Remember that no one is coming to save us. It's not up to me. It's up to you.

About the Author

Cheryl Bonini Ellis, a former business executive-turned-entrepreneur, is the Founder and CEO of Ellis Business Enterprises LLC. She is a trusted advisor to business executives, entrepreneurs and professionals, helping them achieve more and perform at higher levels so that they can get bigger and better results. Her work enabling business leaders to build cohesive, high performing teams supports organizations of all sizes in creating a competitive advantage.

Passionate about personal development, Cheryl works directly with global thought leaders in business growth, leadership excellence, high performance and personal transformation. She combines continuous learning with her own experiences and observations from over forty years of progressive business leadership to provide solutions that work for today's business leaders.

She founded her company to help business leaders achieve better bottom-line results by developing leadership ability at all levels in their organizations. She created the Learning to Lead From Within leadership training series to guide leaders through the tough inside work of leadership. And, she hosts Leading with Impact and Intention, a leadership retreat for women, to encourage and enable women to embrace their personal power to make the world a better place.

She is an active volunteer leader of The Morris County Chamber of Commerce, a Trustee of Morris Arts, dedicated to bringing arts to the center of the community, an avid traveler and amateur photographer.

For more information about other services and programs, visit her websites

www.ellisbusinessenterprises.com

www.johnmaxwellgroup.com/cherylellis

http://about.me/cherylboniniellis

http://cherylboniniellis.brandyourself.com/

Additional Resources

For additional gifts and free resources, visit:

www.BecomingDeliberate.com

And remember to tell a friend about this book!

To receive your free gifts, visit
www.BecomingDeliberate.com
You will be prompted to enter your name & e-mail address
Once entered, click OK to receive your gifts!

http://www.BecomingDeliberate.com